GOD IS MERCIFUL

GOD IS MERCIFUL

The Colorful Career of John E. Egan

DAVID C. GREER

ORANGE *frazer* PRESS
Wilmington, Ohio

ISBN 978-1939710-635

Copyright©2017 David C. Greer

Published for David C. Greer by:

Orange Frazer Press

P.O. Box 214

Wilmington, OH 45177

Telephone: 937.382.3196 for price and shipping information.

Website: www.orangefrazer.com

Book and cover design: Alyson Rua and Orange Frazer Press

Back cover and page 1 photograph: Old Montgomery
County Courthouse, Dayton, Ohio, c. 1902.

Page 7 photograph: Miami-Erie Canal, Ohio.

Pages 14–15 photograph: Union Station, Dayton, Ohio.

Page 75 photograph: Rike's store in downtown Dayton, Ohio, c. 1900s.

Page 105 photograph: Dayton Arcade, Dayton, Ohio.

Library of Congress Control Number: 2017943524

First Printing

Illustration Credits

Cover Artwork by Greg Dearth

Graphic Design by Josh Ogley: Excello, Ohio, Dayton Bar Association Cigar Box, Schwind Building, Union, Ohio, Margaret Collins, Death Row, Egan Grave

Courtesy University of Michigan Bentley Historical Library: 1897 University of Michigan Football Team

Illustrations by Gregoria Garcia: Rose Shafor and Fred Gondorf

Courtesy *Dayton Daily News* Archive: John Dillinger—Dayton Mug Shot

Courtesy Indiana State Archives: Harry Pierpont and Charles Makley Mug Shots

Courtesy Cleveland Press Collection, CSU Michael Schwartz Library: Alvin Karpis Mug Shot

Courtesy National Archives: Dolores Delaney

Contents

GOD IS MERCIFUL

ACT I

Photo portrait of Jack Egan taken in the year of his death.

Entranced and Musing at the Museum Entrance

To the legal scholar the means—the rule of law, the commandments of the Constitution, the play of procedure and precedent—justify the end. There is an old *New Yorker* cartoon that puts this conclusion in an ironic light. Two portly judges in their formal robes are engaged in a corridor chat. One smiles benignly and comments to his equally benign counterpart, "Isn't it nice to have a job where everything you do is by definition justice?" The pin of reality thus pops the balloon of the ideal.

To the client, caught in the net of society or in snares of his own making, the end justifies the means. The sought-for verdict, whether the imposition or avoidance of a money judgment or the gain or loss of personal liberty, is all that counts.

Jack Egan represented countless clients from 1899 to 1936. Their goals were his goals. He was a creature of the earth. During his life he did not inhabit the ivy clad tower of the legal scholar. It is unlikely that he occupied the heights of heaven after his death. His life and local legend is not offered as a model to be admired and followed by lawyers or judges. He was a primal force, viewing the truth as fluid, a substance to sculpt and, at times, pummel into whatever form suited the needs of the particular moment. As he achieved recognition for his forensic skills, he declined an invitation to become a partner of the famed Clarence Darrow. Their careers offer fascinating comparisons and contrasts. In an oblique way, Egan's story—like that of Darrow—does offer moral guidance.

Jack tried his first case, as well as his last case in Dayton's "New" Courthouse that had been built in 1884. That courthouse was demolished half a century ago.

It was across Main Street from the now vacant Third National Building in which Egan had his law office when he transitioned from life to death. As we approach the drama of his thirty-six years at the Dayton Bar, cast an eye on the community in which he strutted and fretted his brief hour upon the stage.

SCENE 1:
A Seedbed of Imagination and Ingenuity

Dayton, Ohio. A city blessed in an increasingly desiccated world with a huge underground aquifer. Set in the center of an area carved by an ancient glacier in the shape of a cereal bowl. A place surrounded by rich farmland. A place where five rivers—the Great Miami, the Stillwater, the Mad River, Wolf Creek, and Twin Creek—meet. Just west of the Shawnee Village of Tecumseh, the great Indian who—but for his brother's mistake—might have built the confederation that blocked the westward expansion of the white man's civilization. A place where, because of the spring flooding of confluent rivers, the Indians were too smart to build the village that was created there by a small group of settlers in 1796.

There must have been something in all that water which stimulated the late nineteenth century and early twentieth century penchant for invention. Whether or not Dayton's water contained some elixir, the fact is that the community during the Egan era contained an extraordinary abundance of inventive and imaginative individuals. The folding stepladder, the first daylight factory, the airplane, the self-starter, ethyl gasoline—the list goes on and on to include finally the best invention since the wheel, the tear-off top of the beer can. The physical and legal engineering that in 1913 stopped the threat of spring floods with the construction of a series of dams which in turn provided the model for the Tennessee Valley Authority and similar projects in the 1930s. The architectural style west of Main

Street/Far Hills south of the central city known as "early General Motors." This was the world in which Jack Egan rose and fell.

Unlike Joyce's Dublin or Faulkner's Oxford, Mississippi, Dayton's spot on the literary stage has been an occasional tiptoe from the wings. The hero of Faulkner's early novel *Sartoris* died in a plane crash in Dayton. The revelers on a train to Spain in Hemingway's *The Sun Also Rises* ran into a group of nuns from the University of Dayton. Eugene Gant's brother in Thomas Wolfe's first novel ended up in the Dayton State Hospital. Some of the characters in John Dos Passos' *U.S.A.* spent an interesting evening in a noted Dayton bordello. The NCR factory and the surrounding houses for its workers made a significant appearance in E. L. Doctorow's *Loon Lake*. The Dayton Air Show is noted in Toni Morrison's novel *Sula*, and the story of a fugitive slave returned from Dayton forms the core of her novel *Beloved*. Kurt Vonnegut's *Slaughterhouse-Five* memorably begins with the observation that Dresden, Germany from the air looks a lot like Dayton, Ohio.

From fiction to fact, the City is the subject of a short, but provocative socialist history of its development written in the 1920s by Joseph Sharts, a Dayton attorney who had represented Eugene Debs in the Pullman strike aftermath. The life of the City in the 1920s is accurately described in a now-forgotten book called *Big Town* written by the brother of the McKee who was a partner in the Dayton law firm of Estabrook, Finn & McKee. The book never mentions Dayton by any other name than Big Town, but it accurately captures the city and its citizens in that vibrant period.

SCENE 2:
Anticipation, Realization, and Catharsis

Our story of a curious and colorful life in that city ends on a beautiful Indian Summer day in August of 1936, six months before the birth of the author of this vicarious reminiscence. An observer placed near a major Catholic church in the heart of the city would have seen a tremendous crowd pressing into and pooling onto the sidewalk outside that crowded edifice. The adjacent street was lined with a seemingly endless row of automobiles awaiting the final ride to Calvary Cemetery. If our observer could have found his way inside, he would have discovered every pew filled with expectant citizens, every aisle filled with members of the congregation who could not find a seat.

The crowd was silent, in hushed attendance at the funeral of a noted Dayton lawyer who in recent years had represented the man J. Edgar Hoover labeled as America's first public enemy number one and who then had the audacity to represent the man who had succeeded to that dubious title. The decedent's reputation was outrageous, but magnetic.

The congregation waited and wondered what the priest would say in the eulogy for the subject of the day's ceremony. There was enough material for a speech that would rival in subject matter and content one of those eight-hour Clarence Darrow closing arguments. In the silence the priest ascended to the pulpit. He paused. He scanned the audience. He bent forward and then stood erect. He spread his arms like angel's wings. He spoke. He said "God is Merciful." He then descended from the pulpit. The attendees quietly left the church.

This little book is intended as a supplement to that eulogy. It is the result of the stories told by lawyers who knew Egan in the decades he spent at the Dayton Bar and of research into written accounts of cases he tried and comments he made.

ACT II

Top right: Excello monument.
Bottom left: Excello lock on the Miami Canal.

A Poet in His Youth

Excello—the site of Jack Egan's birth on August 10, 1873, five months after his father died in March of that year. It is a crossroads mill town at the south end of Middletown, Ohio. It is located a stone's throw west of State Route 4 which runs from the west side of Dayton, through Middletown to Hamilton, Ohio, a city known in the 1920s as Little Chicago since it was part of a lawless county where gangsters came to cool off and where Bix Beiderbecke and his Wolverines offered hot jazz at the Stockton Club. Excello consisted of a large paper plant built at the convergence of the old canal and the Great Miami River. The owner's mansion was across the street from the plant, overlooking a string of cracker box company houses huddled against the roadway which separated the affluent from the deprived.

Excello—the very name is a play on the word "excel." It suggests what Shakespeare in *Macbeth* described as vaulting ambition which o'erleaps itself and falls on the other bank. It doesn't simply mark the site of Egan's birth. It sets the theme of his life. We will revisit *Macbeth* as our narrative unfolds.

SCENE 1:
Pastoral Prelude

Of Jack's fatherless boyhood we know little. Living with his mother, sister, and grandmother, we can imagine him being coddled as the little man of the house. We can look at photos of his surroundings which still exist, the paper mill collapsing upon itself in a ruined state, the president's mansion in restored splendor while the workers' homes remain as a depressing contrast. A boy at play by the old canal where a monument to the Excello lock on the canal remains as a marker for meditation.

We know that the boy rose from his childhood surroundings. Both of his parents had emigrated from Ireland to escape the Great Famine of the 1840s. During the Civil War his father had been a musician with the 126th Regiment, Ohio Infantry, Company D of Ohio Union Volunteers. Thereafter he was listed in census records as a farmer. On his father's death, Jack's mother, Anna, took a housekeeping job at the paper mill to support herself, her two children and her own mother on next to nothing. Jack's older sister, Grace, who was born sometime in late 1870, died in 1894 and was buried next to her father in Middletown, Ohio.

As Jack grew older, he managed to scrape together enough money to attend the National Normal University. When that institution went out of business, he moved on to Miami University, attending classes through 1891 and again in 1895. He then became a school teacher for Butler County in Madison Township in 1893. Although that was a very respectable career, Jack craved more. He began working as a reporter for the *Middletown Daily Signal* where he left a lasting impression of "a brief and brilliant career in journalism." Several years later the *Signal* had more to report: "Jack Egan left last evening for Lima where he has secured a position as a news gatherer for the *Lima News*. Jack is a hustling newspaperman, and the *Lima* reporters will have to get a hump on themselves or a scoop will be a daily occurrence. Jack's many friends here wish him success in his new field of labor."

Jack emerges from the mist of his boyhood in 1896 when he was admitted to the University of Michigan Law School. It was here that the spark of ambition caught fire. He was quickly caught up in the University's social, academic and athletic life. He retained his membership in the Sigma Chi fraternity, having previously pledged at Miami University. In his college summers he continued his work as an energetic reporter for the daily newspaper in Lima, Ohio, where many years later the sheriff would be killed while trying to keep one of Jack's clients confined.

SCENE 2:
Aggression and Aspiration

In 1897 Jack was a guard on the University of Michigan football team which finished the season in a 6-1-1 record. He became the president of his senior law class in 1899. The photograph of the formidable-looking, thirteen-man football team depicts a serious young man with an intimidating glare and a firmly set jaw. The photograph of him at the center of six of his graduating law school classmates reflects the same steely determination in a high collar, academic pose.

Egan's address as president of the University of Michigan Senior Law School class at its graduation in 1899 has been preserved. It reflects the pious aspirations of the man and of his era.

> It is our great advantage to be living in the greatest age, in the greatest country of the civilized world. It has been truthfully said that America is but another word for opportunity, and in this great democratic nation 'hope is the tailor of every ragged boy.' In our chosen profession, there is a place for merit and worth. Sons of genius and toil are

11

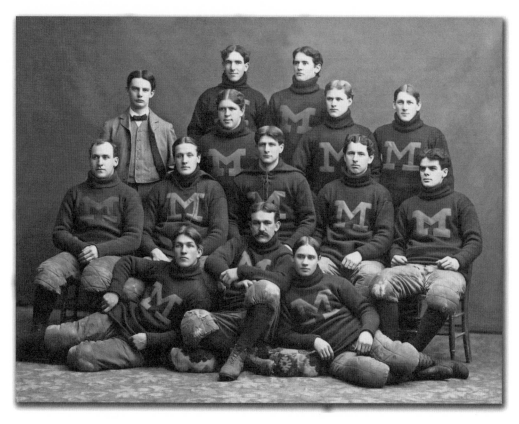

1897 University of Michigan football team. Egan is in the second row, second from right.

always gladly received, and well compensated. From the class of laws about to graduate, it can be safely said, there are many men who are destined to be prominent in the councils of the nation.

His concept of American liberty had no relationship to the freeing of guilty criminals from the bulwarks of American penitentiaries.

As students of the law we have learned to appreciate its force and reason, and if we are not great lawyers, we will surely be better citizens. We will always be associated with the conservative element in government, and in our weak way and manner each man shall put forth his best effort to make our profession in the future what it has always been in the past—one of the bulwarks of American liberty.

His speech ended on a high and prophetic note.

Let us all live so that we will have no trouble to obtain our life credits. Let the world say of us, he has been a faithful servant, let those who know us best and love us most say he has fought a good fight and the world is better for his having lived.

University of Michigan Law School class of 1899. Egan as Class President.

Like Macbeth in Act I, he emerged from the fields of physical and mental battle prepared to ascend to higher honors and more impressive achievements.

13

ACT III

Dayton Bar Association cigar box with portraits of Dayton lawyers. (Egan at upper left; Nevin at upper right; Baggott at lower left; Sprigg at lower right.)

The Dyer's Hand

Springing from the platform of platitudes contained in his law school commencement speech, Jack arrived in Dayton to launch his career in the law. Unlike Macbeth, he did not have to kill a king to reach the throne, and there were no ravens croaking themselves hoarse as he made his fatal entrance to the Union Station on Sixth Street. In later years, however, he frequently commented on the role of fate in the decision he made when he arrived at Sixth and Main.

He walked north on the east side of Main Street. Just before reaching the Victory Theatre at the corner of First and Main he turned right and stepped into Eve and Dick Williams' saloon. There he met three young Dayton attorneys—Roland Baggott, Jake Nevin and Caroll Sprigg. Drinks were consumed and friendships were formed. "Those lawyers in that bar," claimed Egan, "turned me into the kind of a son-of-a-bitch I am. If I had walked up the west side of Main Street and turned left at the same place I turned right, I would have been in the First Baptist Church and turned into a great lawyer like Oscar Gottschall!" We are known by the company we keep, and—as the author of *Tristram Shandy* teaches—good stories often move sideways while they are trying to move forward.

Oscar Gottschall was the archetype of the perfect corporate lawyer—impeccable in appearance, dignified, reliable, industrious, a model of honor and trustworthiness. He came to the Bar in 1866 after serving as a lieutenant in the Union Army through major Civil War battles in which he was twice wounded. The boys in the bar were considerably younger, considerably more relaxed, considerably more convivial, each possessed with a sense of humor and the common touch.

Caroll Sprigg had been a football star at Yale. He later served as a common pleas judge from 1910 to 1917 when he became President Wilson's Ambassador to Egypt. After that tour of duty he practiced law in Dayton until his death in 1942. Robert "Jake" Nevin was the son of a gregarious Dayton attorney who had a half circle cut in his dining room table to accommodate his bulk. Jake joined his father in the practice of law in 1898. In 1901, he was the first president of the Dayton Bar Association. In 1905, he served as the county prosecuting attorney. In 1929, he was appointed as the first resident judge to sit in the Federal District Court in Dayton. He was gifted with wit, humor and an understanding of human nature. Poets in their youth, these two cronies of young Jack Egan followed careers quite different from his.

The third young lawyer Jack met on that fateful day in Eve and Dick Williams' saloon also followed the path to a courthouse. Roland Baggott was a unique individual, a man of wit and considered the funniest man at the Dayton Bar. He never lost his playful sense of life and his delight in the human comedy. While he followed Jake Nevin and Caroll Sprigg from bar to bench, he remained—as we shall see—a crony of Jack Egan as they both traveled from the start to the conclusion of their professional careers. His uncle had been a Montgomery County probate judge in the 1840s; his sons would become Dayton lawyers in 1929; his grandson is still fully engaged in the practice of law in Dayton as these lines are being written in 2016. In 1908, Baggott became Montgomery County's probate judge. His judicial roles expanded with time and new legislation. He became Montgomery County's first juvenile court judge and its first domestic relations judge. He gave it all up in 1926 and returned to the private practice of law where after a few years he was joined by his sons. His son, Horace, known as "Hop," became a notable trial lawyer. During his high school years Hop worked as an office boy in Jack Egan's office. One of his early assignments was to carry a message to the nuns. When he arrived at the nunnery, he was surprised to find out that it was the bordello owned and operated by Dayton's famous Lib Hedges where the habits of the girls were definitely not nuns' habits.

A Pearl Street nunnery.

Until recent years, long after the passing of Jack's era in the practice of law, it was inappropriate, unethical and sanctionable for a lawyer to self-promote with advertising of any kind. A name on the door or a group picture, however, did not go over the limit. If you are lucky enough to find an old Dayton Bar cigar box at a flea market, lift the lid and you will find all four of these refugees from Eve and Dick Williams' saloon as well as a number of their fellow lawyers.

The three barristers Jack encountered in that saloon in the fine old days of the Dayton Bar were not Macbeth's witches stirring some cauldron of chaos. They may have contributed to Egan's sense of humor, his empathy for the all-too-human-beings he encountered, and his slightly jaded view that all life is a game put in play for a knowing participant's personal amusement. But they cannot be held accountable for transforming him into the son-of-a-bitch he readily admitted to being. Although he died the year before I was born, Jack remains as vividly alive to me as anyone I encounter on my daily trip through this transitory existence. If his character was not forged and formed by his chance encounter in a Dayton saloon, was it the product of nature and nurture provided by his family?

SCENE 1:
Distressed and Distressing Damsels

While Jack's image remains clear, the images of his mother, his sister and his spouse are blurred by the paucity of contemporary recollections. The only boy in a fatherless home is likely to secure some special attention and to develop a sense that the world turns around him. There is nothing to magnetize a mother's love like a son who is something of a rascal. A struggling sister is likely to view a brother as a protector to be placed on an imaginary pedestal. A boy growing up in such an atmosphere can be predicted to have a strong self-image and to become a dominant husband. The 1900 census shows Jack living in a boarding house in Dayton while his mother is still living in Excello. By April of 1910, Jack was living with his mother on West Fourth Street in Dayton. By May he appears to have married Ellen "Nellie" Ford and to be living with her and her brother George in an apartment on Main Street. Nellie will outlive Jack by twenty years.

These sketchy family facts leave the explanation of Jack's personality as elusive as ever. They may, however, throw some light on the ambition and aspirational idealism reflected in Jack's law school commencement speech. And, despite some subsequent misdirection of that ambition and deflation of that idealism, they may foreshadow a penchant Jack displayed throughout his career for serving as a protector of womanhood. In his own unusual way he was always ready to rescue a damsel in distress, although most of those damsels had already created their own distress before Jack met them.

An early example of this characteristic took place before the automobile replaced the horse and buggy on Ohio roadways. The fair maiden in need of a chivalrous knight was Mary Hirsch. The fact that she was a member of the notorious Spohr gang of burglars and shoplifters who had been terrorizing the county in 1903 did not diminish her plight. She had been arrested in Dayton by a marshal from Franklin and taken to jail in Lebanon awaiting action by a grand jury on a charge of receiving stolen goods from other members of the gang who had already been tried and convicted for a Franklin burglary. Jack to the rescue. Through a writ of habeas corpus he pursued his client's release, put her in a buggy, and began driving as fast as he could to get her over the north county line of Warren County.

As soon as Jack and Mary left the Lebanon jail, the Warren County Sheriff showed up with another warrant for her arrest. It was a race that rivaled the excitement generated by Ben Hur on the silent screen. For Jack and Mary it was a race for freedom. For the sheriff it was a race for justice. Justice had the better horse. Jack was overtaken. His passenger was returned in triumph to the Warren County Jail. Bloody but unbowed, Jack—according to the newspaper account of the affair—was a little disgusted, but still had his hat in the ring. Even more unfortunately, however, Mary's residence was later found to be filled with stolen goods, and her round trip in a horse and buggy ended in a conviction.

In 1911, Jack tried to help another lady with a writ of habeas corpus and again ran into an unfortunate outcome. His client was the mother of a sixteen-year-old girl named Bessie Beatty who had been born as Bessie Lamb. When her parents were divorced, she went to live with the Beatty family in a small Ohio village. Her mother ultimately remarried and began yearning for her daughter's love and companionship. Jack to the rescue. He obtained a writ of habeas corpus, and on a pleasant Sunday morning he and the sheriff arrived at the Beatty home to reunite mother and daughter.

Mr. Beatty presented a revolver and informed Jack and the sheriff that their health would be better served if they simply left the county. Jack began to present a profound legal argument, but the child announced that she was as anxious to remain with the Beattys as the Beattys were to have Jack and the sheriff leave the county without her. By that time a hostile mob had gathered and the tension in the little village had escalated. The sheriff and Jack went to the county seat, but the county sheriff refused to enforce the writ. Jack went home without a sixteen-year-old companion, and it is doubtful that the girl's mother received a Mother's Day card the following May.

In 1907, between his two uneventful forays with writs of habeas corpus on behalf of ladies in distress, Jack had the experience of representing a truly innocent lady. Between 1900 and 1910 there was a series of rape/murders of young Dayton girls which shared a common *modus operandi*. The crimes were described in feverous journalese as the work of a fiendish man-gorilla who strangled his victims after raping them. Only one of those cases ever resulted in an actual trial. Jack was not involved in that trial. Perhaps he should have been. In retrospect it seems clear that the defendant was simply an innocent scapegoat who was wrongfully convicted of a crime he did not commit. Like the other murders in the series, that one should have simply passed into the realm of impenetrable and unsolved mystery.

The 1907 victim of the man-gorilla was a young Jewish girl named Anna Markowitz. In the immediate aftermath of her assault and murder, the young man who had been in her company was shot and killed. In the law enforcement desperation of unsolved murders and with a tinge of the anti-Semitism prevailing at the time, Anna's sister Bertha and her two brothers were arrested and jailed on suspicion. Jack came to the rescue, and this time his writ of habeas corpus worked. Anna's siblings were freed to grieve over their loss, and they were never prosecuted for acts of which they were clearly innocent. It was in fact Jack who first pointed out that the characteristics of the murder of Anna Markowitz were identical to those of the previous murder of Donna Gilman, a murder that remained unsolved. The issue of who shot the young man who was with Anna at the time of her assault was left unexplored in the public excitement about the man-gorilla who apparently was still at large and putting the young girls of Dayton at risk.

In his last days, Jack was engaged to seek freedom for another damsel in distress, a lady by the name of Dolores Delaney. That effort was unfortunately not a success. The retention of Jack's services came from Alvin Karpis who at the time had succeeded John Dillinger as America's Public Enemy Number One. That story will appear in a later chapter. There is, however, a heartwarming story of another damsel in distress who was restored to happiness by Jack's efforts on her behalf. As the curious twists and turns of Jack's life would have it, however, that distressed damsel was not his client. Jack was representing her husband in a divorce action, and the damsel was a client of Jack's opponent in that saga of domestic intranquility.

A local banker had become estranged from his wife of many years and had also become infatuated with a young lady as loose of morals as she was tight of pulchritude. While the banker was not a typical Egan client, his paramour was the archetypal Egan client. The banker came to Egan for the divorce that would hopefully pave his way to a life of erotic bliss. Judge Baggott had retired from the bench, and the banker's wife had come to his office with a tearful tale of her husband's infidelity. She told the ex-judge that she loved her philandering husband, that she had taken care of him from the time he started with the bank at $25 per week, that she cleaned for him, that she cooked for him, that she had raised his family, and that she had never raised her voice. In fact, she said, she loved him so much that if he really wanted a divorce she would let him have it and ask for nothing.

Egan received a call from his old crony and heard this tale in its unvarnished form. He then called in the banker client and told him that the wife had gone to ex-judge Baggott, that those judges stick together, and that at Baggott's request the present judge was likely to make an award of alimony which would put the banker back at the $25 per week level of income to call his own. "Do you think you and your new girlfriend can live on $25 a week?" asked Egan. "Oh, no," replied the client, "I wouldn't ask her to do that." "Well," said Egan, "that's your alternative; you can either call off the divorce or live on $25 a week with your new girlfriend."

A few weeks later Judge Baggott's client came to him all wreathed in smiles. Her husband had begged her forgiveness. He didn't want the divorce. He wanted to live with her until the end of his days. She was overjoyed. Jack Egan, the unlikely cupid in his renewed romance, is said to have charged the banker the handsome sum of $1,000 for the aborted divorce. When the client complained that the fee sounded like a lot of money, Jack told him to look for a whore instead of a lawyer the next time he got sexually aroused. "It's cheaper."

Did Jack achieve the best result for his banker client? Or did two old cronies simply play a joke for the betterment of both clients? And what about the floozy who had probably referred the banker to Jack in the first place and who ended up as the real loser in the affair? Jack probably rationalized her outcome with the thought that she undoubtedly landed on her feet (or seat). For a good gal like that, rich sugar daddies are like street cars. If you miss one, there will always be another one along shortly.

The cozy relationship between Egan and Baggott almost led to tragedy in a domestic relations case that unfolded while Baggott was still on the bench. This time Jack did represent the damsel in distress. She had lost the custody of her two small children when her hot-headed German husband succeeded in obtaining a divorce by proving that she had engaged in adultery. Imagine Jack representing a woman like that! After she married the adulterer, Jack continued to represent her and took her back to Judge Baggott's court where an order was entered returning the custody of her children to her.

On a Saturday morning when Judge Baggott was holding court, the ex-husband stormed into the office of his own attorney waving a revolver and announcing that he was going to kill the judge and then go to Egan's office and finish him off as well. His lawyer could not dissuade him from his mission, and he stormed out the door with the revolver in his hand. Happily the lawyer called Judge Baggott's bailiff who, with the help of a sheriff's deputy, overcame the angry ex-husband as he reached the top of the courthouse stairs. He probably wasn't the last human being who thought about killing Jack, but at least Jack's lady client had succeeded in snatching victory (and the possession of her children) out of the jaws of defeat.

Did Jack have some Don Quixote kind of thing when it came to women? There is ample evidence to support a negative answer to this question. Consider his excoriating cross-examinations of women who appeared as adverse witnesses in his cases. Forgotten was the graceful and civilized tone of chivalric gentility; tears were of no avail; the gates of mercy were slammed shut in the ruthless quest for the desired admission. And consider the sad case of Minnie Miller. In 1904, Jack represented her husband in a divorce action in the course of which he discovered that she had three other un-divorced husbands and a fourth un-divorced husband who was resting in a graveyard. Did he counsel his client to forgive and forget? No. He had poor Minnie arrested and sent to jail for bigamy.

And what about that doctor he represented in 1906, who held a lady and her newborn baby hostage until her husband paid him his bill for his obstetrical services? The poor husband was arrested on a charge of defrauding an innkeeper. He had to post a bond to cover the doctor's bill. Even after he subsequently kidnapped his wife and newborn child from the hospital and filed an affidavit charging the doctor with cruelty for detaining the mother and child against the bill as well as against her will, he was arrested a second time. So much for Jack's reverence for the fair sex and motherhood.

And what about that writ of replevin Jack filed on behalf of the Olds Motor Company in 1910, alleging misconduct by a handsome young woman of a type he should have admired? She had visited a car agency in Chicago and, when being taken for a demonstration ride, suggested to the salesman that they stop at a certain restaurant for lunch. When the salesman stepped inside the restaurant to arrange the lunch, an acquaintance of the lady jumped into the car and drove away with her and the machine at the highest speed the machine could muster. The car was thereafter sold to the owner of a Dayton foundry. Upon its discovery Jack was engaged to represent its rightful owner. The old newspapers don't explain how Jack learned of the scam.

Neither Nevin, Sprigg nor Baggott can be blamed for Jack Egan's flawed but colorful personality and character. Only Shakespeare could do him justice and produce the longed-for explanation. He did so in Sonnet 111:

> O! for my sake do you with Fortune chide,
> The guilty goddess of my harmful deeds,
> That did not better for my life provide
> Than public means which public manners breeds.

Thence comes it that my name receives a brand;

And almost thence my nature is subdued

To what it works in, like the dyer's hand.

Instead of finding a perch on a bench of justice like the friends he met in that Dayton saloon or of finding a pious sanctuary in the church across the street, Jack dove headfirst into the ocean of crime and corruption that provides the element in which a defense lawyer must swim. Most of those who follow that branch of this honorable profession do so with integrity. I often remind myself fondly of a notable criminal defense lawyer from Canada who made it clear that he would represent any fellow human being charged with any crime, no matter how heinous the crime or how loud the public hue and cry. But he would only represent any client once. A second representation of the same client might blur the sharp distinction between the lawyer's role and the client's conduct. Thus is the risk avoided that the dyer's hand becomes colored by the element in which it works.

SCENE 2:
Citizens of Cockroach Castle

Jack Egan became immersed in Dayton's underworld almost as soon as he left Eve and Dick Williams' saloon on the day of his arrival in Dayton. Sightings of him in 1900 disclose a high-spirited young man ready to impress his peers and make a name for himself. In March, the Sons of St. Patrick—a group that included a number of Dayton lawyers and judges—had a big banquet at the Phillips House, the old hotel at the southwest corner of Third and Main streets where Lincoln had stayed in 1859 and where the Dayton Lawyers Club would be formed in 1909. The hit of the evening was Jack's "spirited and earnest talk that appealed to the enthusiasm of all." In June, he was involved in the trial of a divorce case in which it was impossible to tell which spouse was more despicable. It was reported as affording considerable amusement around the courthouse, and a denial of the divorce was predicted based on the indisputable fact that neither party had come to equity with clean hands.

By the summer of 1900, Jack had become a regular participant in the sordid affairs that were the routine grist of the police court mill. He was observed to evoke "considerable merriment" in prosecuting a *pro se* defendant for violating the city health ordinance in a manner politely left unrecorded by the press. In the same summer the ambitious subject of this work was offering free legal services in a situation involving a poker game between certain public officials and certain local businessmen.

The picture painted by his clients in 1901 began to have less in common with Fragonard than with Hieronymus Bosch. Jack was still magnetized to the human comedy, but he was no longer giving his services away for nothing. James Parr, whose wife had run off with a son of the King of the Gypsies, desperately needed Jack's services. He really didn't want his wife back under the circumstances, but he did not want his little daughter, Mabel, to grow up in the wild camp of the gypsies. Twice Jack found the ever-moving camp, but Parr was short of the money needed to reach his goal.

Jack was almost lured into taking a case for a heavily bandaged client who gave him a story of being trapped under a freight car of the Big Four Railroad on a run between Columbus and Cincinnati. When Jack went to see Jake Nevin who represented the Big Four, however, he discovered that the bandages only covered the nakedness of a fraudulent rascal who had made the same injury claim through other counsel. Jack was nonetheless still ready, willing, and ever eager to assert claims wherever there was a claim to be made and a fee to be paid. And he was always busy with his ever-ready habeas corpus writs to pull clients out of the workhouse. In the case of Charlie Jordan, the client had the indignity of being thrown into the workhouse while he was out on bond for two other criminal offenses. Being "out" was his desire and the desire of every client.

The old police court was located on Sixth Street east of the canal. It became unusable after the 1913 flood. As a result of legislation that year, it was combined with the old justice of the peace courts and moved to the second floor of the market house which ran from Main Street to Jefferson Street a short distance south of Third Street. At that time it became the Dayton Municipal Court. William Budroe who became a Dayton lawyer in 1904 was the judge of the police court until 1913 when he became the first chief judge of the three-man Dayton Municipal Court, a position he held until his death in 1921.

During the first two decades of Jack Egan's career, Judge Budroe and Jack were in almost daily contact. Like Jack, he had a colorful personality. While Jack may have prided himself on being a son-of-a-bitch, Judge Budroe once added $100 to a defendant's fine when the defendant reacted to the initial fine for his offense by calling the Judge a son-of-a-bitch in open court. The unhappy defendant who had been fined for exercising his right of free speech asked the court if he could be fined for simply thinking. Judge Budroe said "No." Thereupon the

City police court and jail 1873–1913 on south side of Sixth Street just west of Tecumseh Street ("Cockroach Castle").

defendant said, "Well, I still think you're a son-of-a-bitch!"

The old police court and city jail was commonly referred to as Cockroach Castle, and in those not-so-golden days of social and racial prejudice the clients Jack represented in that court received more derision than respect. A news article in 1906 described the police court as "a most interesting zoo" containing "a costly collection captured in the wilds of the Bungaloo and the wastes of Western Avenue." The task of the court was described as

City municipal court and jail 1913–1953 on east side of Main Street between Third and Fourth streets.

training vicious dogs into a social semblance of docility and programming wild birds "not to fly around their old roosting places anymore." The police court bailiff was quoted as introducing the assembled defendants as members of "the monkey family every one of which has during the past twenty-four hours made a monkey of himself." His introduction was concluded with the comment that "the entire bunch will be taken at once to Sixth and the railroad, our summer and winter quarters," the site of the city workhouse. Jack's labors in that environment were not for the faint-hearted.

The Bungaloo was a notorious building at the corner of Second Street and Clinton Street, a location which—like Pearl Street which ran from Wayne Avenue to East Fifth Street and housed Lib Hedges' bordello and the rest of Dayton's famous red light district—no longer exists. The "wilds" of the Bungaloo were described by the press in glowing terms:

> I would state that this district is considered one of the most dangerous in all Montgomery County. It is inhabited by vari-colored peoples, representing mixed races. The capture of anything there is only undertaken with great peril.

29

The "wastes" of Western Avenue, now known as James H. McGee Boulevard, were on the west side of the city, running south to north past the City Railway car barn and the Sucher meat-packing plant.

Another news article reported Egan's ingenuity in using that mixed race issue to defend some Bungaloo inhabitants. An evening of free pigtails and sauerkraut had been advertised at the Bungaloo, and the place was packed with happy participants in the feast. A police raid occurred, resulting in white citizens being told to go home and not to mix with black citizens. The raid also resulted in the arrest of three black women for loitering. Egan arrived in police court with a large throng of the black women who had been enjoying the evening in question, and the arresting officer was unable to identify which three of the group he had arrested. Whoever they were, they were released.

Presumably the same fascinated news reporter provided a later account of a "big session" in police court featuring Jack Egan's representation of Kate Wambo on a charge of keeping a disorderly house on Springfield Street. Since prostitution until 1915 was perfectly legal in Dayton's red light district, her only crime appears to have been carrying out her trade in the wrong location. Four male defendants in court that day were fined for encouraging a disorderly house, and a lady named Esther Maddox was found guilty of being a common character, a euphemism that could accurately be applied to everyone present, including the lawyers and the judge. The hazards of the defense lawyers' trade are reflected in the conviction of a defendant in the same court session for stealing Jack Egan's watch.

On another occasion Egan is described as arriving at Cockroach Castle to defend three female members of the half-world for getting into a fight in front of Sapp's Place on West Fifth Street. Before he arrived in court, the girls had already pled guilty, paid their fines, and departed for Sapp's in a wagon singing "Wait 'Til The Sun Shines, Nellie." A last sample of the high respect accorded Jack's typical clientele and the daily proceedings at the Cockroach Castle is provided by a news article describing in extremely poor taste the court proceedings as a bigger and livelier vaudeville show than could be found in any theater. Songs are ascribed to each of the courtroom participants. Moses Jones, Dayton's first black attorney, is listed as singing "There's Nothing Like This In My Family." "I Don't See No Room For An Argument" is Jack Egan's song. Various lady defendants of ill repute are described as singing such features as "Hanging Around" and "Can't You See I'm Lonely."

If all this sounds like something out of a Eugene O'Neill play, the only excuse that can be offered is that—just as art imitates life—life imitates art.

SCENE 3:
The Gang's All Here

In February of 1901, Egan was chosen to represent the perfect client. Unlike that Canadian lawyer who would only represent a defendant once, a member of Dayton's criminal defense bar a generation after the Egan era was asked why the same defendants and all their family members and friends kept engaging his services despite the fact that they all ended up in the penitentiary. His answer was that all those people knew the system and knew that their conduct violated the law and that the system was rigged against them whether or not they violated the law. Those clients all shared the need and desire simply to have someone who would stand up and fight and speak on their behalf. If that need and desire is satisfied, the outcome is irrelevant. A client who is in constant trouble with the law is a client who is in constant need of a lawyer. If the client can pay for legal services, he is a client on whom the lawyer can rely to support his professional practice. Andrew Spohr was such a client.

In February of 1901, Spohr was arrested in Cincinnati as one of a group of men who had burglarized the Peters Arms and Sporting Goods Company of that city. When arrested he had a knife that was identified as having been taken from the store. Jack Egan to the rescue. He headed to Cincinnati with a list of eighteen witnesses who could support the alibi that Spohr was in bed in Dayton when the burglary occurred in Cincinnati. How eighteen people happened to be in Spohr's bedroom on a Saturday night was left unexplained, but a continuing attorney-client bond was formed. It was calculated that the cost of the witnesses alone, if all eighteen were taken to Cincinnati, would be $126.00.

In April, Jack tried to obtain a continuance of Andy Spohr's trial on the ground that some of the women he intended to call as witnesses "were not the best of character and drifted from one place to another." In response, Ulysses S. Martin, the prosecutor, went with police officers to Middletown to take depositions of those women. Two were found in Middletown. Another was found in a roadhouse. One was found in the back room of a saloon drinking and having what is politely described as a good time. The newspaper reported that "she was glad to learn that her evidence and not herself was wanted by the Dayton officers." Jack was in his element!

When Andy Spohr's case came to trial in late April of 1901, prosecutor Martin, Judge Oren B. Brown, Jack Egan, and a panel of prospective jurors were all present in court. Spohr, however, did not show up. Jack, who had unsuccessfully tried to get a change of venue based on public prejudice against his client, professed to have no knowledge of Spohr's whereabouts. A search team was sent from the sheriff's office without success. Spohr apparently had decided that if he couldn't change the venue of his case, he could at least change the venue of himself.

In November of 1901, Spohr was arrested again, this time for a Dayton burglary. He was spotted by the police when he and two of his cronies stepped off an incoming Southern Ohio traction car at Sixth and Main streets in downtown Dayton. The news report described Spohr as the "most notorious" of the group and noted that he had been arrested for many crimes, including the murder of a butcher in the course of a robbery. It also noted that he always managed to "wriggle out." There was a chase. Spohr and his cronies were shortly thereafter apprehended in a Fifth Street restaurant. Some of the stolen property was recovered in an alley running from Ludlow Street south of the railroad. More business for Jack Egan.

A few weeks later the Dayton Police attempted a "clean sweep" of the burglars known as the Spohr gang. Fifty-two people were arrested and locked in the station house for investigation. At that point Egan had a full deck of clients. Conflicts of interest were not a popular legal topic at the time, and we will find him throughout his career representing multiple clients charged with the same or related criminal conduct. As a side note, one of the victims of the burglaries covered by the sweep was a businessman-attorney named Henry Hollencamp who would become the father, grandfather and great-grandfather of Dayton attorneys.

By January of 1902, Jack was back in court with a writ of habeas corpus for Charles Meyers, one of the Spohr gang who had been arrested in the November "clean sweep." Meyers had been released on bail. Shortly thereafter he was hospitalized with typhoid fever. His health was starting to return when the police showed up at St. Elizabeth Hospital and rearrested him. Back in jail at 4:00 on a Friday afternoon, he was—thanks to Jack—once again a free man on bail by 6:00 p.m. on Saturday.

The Spohr gang continued to thrive, with or without Andy. In November of 1902, a pair of bloodhounds tracked a shipment of coffee stolen from a boxcar to a corn field where the coffee was hidden. The dogs then took the scent from the tracks left by a buggy that had delivered the coffee to the corn field, and they led the police to the Spohr residence on Charles Street near South Park in Dayton. There the police found Andy's brother, Charles, and two other men. Also in the room were two of Andy's sisters and a lot of the stolen coffee. The men were arrested for burglary and larceny. All five were represented in court by Attorney Jack Egan.

In late December of 1902, members of the gang—Andy's brother, Lewis "Skinny" Spohr, Doc Brinkman and three women, each of whom had a dozen aliases, were arrested in Cincinnati for burglaries and shoplifting. The news report indicated that Andy Spohr was still the leader of the gang and that he had been suspected of the murder of an old man. Skinny and others of the gang were arrested again in January of 1903 for burglary and shoplifting in Franklin, Ohio.

During 1902, the Spohr gang had gradually been replaced by the Cook gang (later called the Bunglaoo gang) as the most notorious nest of scoundrels in the City of Dayton. As the baton passed from client to client, the attorney for the reigning felons remained the same. In mid-November of 1903, the police surprised Frank Cook and one of his gang members at the house of a lady known as Rose Zimmerman. Cook was shot in the arm and thrown in jail after being taken to a hospital.

Jack Egan represented Cook at his arraignment on burglary and larceny charges. The jail physician indicated that Cook was in no danger of losing his life from the bullet wound. He opined, however, that Cook might be in danger of losing his arm if not transferred back to the hospital. Frank continued to lead his gang until June of 1908, when he arrived at the Ohio State Penitentiary to serve a five-year sentence for breaking into a boxcar and stealing a quantity of valuable merchandise. The gang was aptly described as a band of thugs and murderers who had terrorized the City of Dayton for years.

Egan added others to his growing clientele in 1903, but Frank Cook passed Andy Spohr at the top of the list until an alleged murderer who was part of the Cook gang was transported from Denver to Dayton on April 30 of that year.

Old Courthouse 1850–present and New Courthouse 1884–1966
on west side of Main Street between Second and Third streets.

SCENE 4:

The Saga of Dayton Slim

On July 23, 1904, Jack was traveling by train from Columbus to Dayton. Seated next to him was an attractive lady named Rose Shafor. In another car on the same train was the body of his client Charles Stimmel, also known as Dayton Slim, who had been electrocuted at the Ohio State Penitentiary the previous night. Rose was the sister of Frank Cook and the other core members of the infamous Cook gang. In 1903, she had fallen in love with Stimmel who was part of that gang. She left her husband to become his paramour.

Every young trial lawyer dreams of the big case that will throw him into the theatre of the courtroom, into the spotlight of public fascination, and into the role of the go-to attorney who gets the first call from every citizen who finds himself in trouble with the law. The trial of Dayton Slim in December of 1903, provided that moment for Jack. Like the great battle that opens the drama of *Macbeth*, it demonstrated that his nature had indeed become subdued to the element in which he worked. And, even if he did not unseam his adversaries from the nave to the chops, he had fixed his hand upon the battlements and become the Thane of Cawdor as far as the Dayton Bar was concerned. His participation in the events leading to, through, and beyond that trial thus justify detailed scrutiny.

Newspaper sketch of Charles Stimmel (Dayton Slim).

Newspaper sketch of Joseph Shide.

The story begins on November 22, 1902, at Allen and Eminger's Feed Store on Wayne Avenue. In the office are four men, two employees of the store and two men who don't belong there. The employees are Joseph Shide and William R. Fishbach. The others are a tall man wearing a black slouch hat and a shorter man. Both had masks from under their eyes to the lower part of their chins. The tall man had a revolver in his right hand. The shorter man had a revolver in each hand. The employees had been loading and unloading cars at the grain elevator adjacent to the store. They were met in the driveway as they went from the elevator to the store. As the four of them went into the office, Shide was following Fishbach and was followed in turn by the tall masked man and by the shorter masked man.

After they had taken several steps into the office the tall man shot Shide in the leg. Shide said, "oh my leg," and he continued to move toward the office safe. At that point the tall man shot him in the back and killed him. The shorter man had both his revolvers trained on Fishbach who, in turn, had his hands in the air. The tall man asked Fishbach for the keys to the safe. Fishbach complied, and the masked man tried without success to open the safe. The office was so dark that he had to strike a match to see when he tried to fit the key to the safe. He then took Shide's pocketbook out of the dead man's pocket and, with his companion, left the office while they kept Fishbach covered with their revolvers.

On August 30, 1903, Dayton detectives McBride and Neidergall brought Charles Stimmel to Dayton from Denver, Colorado, where he had been living with Rose Shafor under assumed names as husband and wife for four months. Rose later followed him to Dayton. The murder trial of Charles Stimmel began on December 9, 1903, and ended when a guilty verdict was returned at 10:30 p.m. on Christmas Eve, December 24, 1903. It was a major event in the Dayton community which had been and continued to be beset with what the Dayton newspapers described at the outset of the trial as an epidemic of crime in which crooks entertain but little fear because of loose police control. "Not a night passes," noted the *Dayton Daily News* on December 9, 1903, "that there are not one or more burglaries." The trial was closely followed by the press and by the public. It killed Charles Stimmel, but it gave birth to the legendary reputation of Jack Egan.

The events leading up to the trial and the events between the verdict and the execution are as noteworthy as the trial itself. Rose Shafor, the lady on the train with Egan on the ride to Dayton from the death house in July of 1904, was well documented in the local press as "the consort of thugs and murderers and the most notorious woman in the Miami Valley." She had come to Dayton with her parents in the 1880s

and progressed from a wayward child to a street-walking prostitute to part of the notorious Cook band of burglars and safecrackers. When the murder which led to Dayton Slim's arrest, conviction and punishment occurred, there was speculation that she was wearing men's clothes and participated in the burglary during which the murder took place. It is clear that after the murder, she and Stimmel went to a boarding house in Springfield, Ohio. Dayton detectives obtained leads that led them to that boarding house after Stimmel had left Springfield and traveled to New Orleans.

A detective was planted at the boarding house to become familiar with Rose,

Newspaper sketch of Rose Shafor.
Sketch from photo.

and other detectives were stationed as observers across the street. The detectives intercepted a letter which Rose sent to her lover at General Delivery in New Orleans. Stimmel was smart enough to send a surrogate to pick up his mail. When the surrogate was stopped by police at the New Orleans post office, Stimmel headed off to Denver, Colorado. Torn between her young son in Dayton and her lover in Denver, Rose subsequently joined Stimmel in Denver. Her communications with her son were intercepted by the detectives and ultimately led to the discovery of the couple's Denver address. It was pretty effective detective work for Dayton in 1903, a world in which most crimes, including murders, went unsolved.

A preliminary hearing was held on September 4, 1903, before Squire Terry who was permitted to use the Common Pleas Courtroom because of the interest aroused by the case. As expected, Jack Egan was there to represent the defendant.

Pause, dear Reader. Slip your feet into Jack Egan's shoes and tiptoe into the criminal justice system as it existed over one hundred years ago. Until you came on the scene your client had no right to counsel or to be advised of such a right. The typical approach to the preparation of a criminal prosecution was to cajole or beat a confession or a pack of easily demonstrateable lies out of the lips of a suspect who was often a mere scapegoat. There was no discovery available to a defendant or to his lawyer in a criminal case. A lawyer had to live by his wits and by his native eloquence to combat whatever the state's witnesses might say in a truly adversarial system which was designed by the somewhat flawed theory that in the clash of self-interest the truth would emerge. Defense counsel and potential jurors got their information through word of mouth and newspaper articles which often provided much gossip and innuendo. Such information was then filtered through subjectivity and prejudice to take whatever form it might take in the minds of those who would defend the accused or decide his life or death. The rules of professional ethics, both for prosecutors and defense counsel, were still in a state of embryonic development. The defendant had a single goal—liberty and an escape from jail, the penitentiary, and the death cell. For the defendant the desired end justified whatever means it took to reach that goal.

The only sneak preview you had as defense counsel, aside from what your client and his witnesses—if any—told you, was a preliminary hearing at which the state was required to disclose the bare minimum of information to justify taking the case to a grand jury. The State's grand jury presentation would be a secret proceeding to which neither the defendant nor his counsel would have access or input. When the grand jury, after hearing only the prosecutor's side of the story, returns an indictment, you as defense counsel go to trial on behalf of a fellow human being who is branded with the name "defendant" and has the hue and cry of a media-aroused lynch mob ringing in his ears. What could be more fun than that?

Ulysses S. Martin was the prosecutor who handled the Stimmel preliminary hearing and who would subsequently handle the grand jury and trial. He came to the Bar in 1894 and had been the county prosecutor since 1899. He would become a Common Pleas judge in 1905, and he had a son, Robert, who would serve as a Common Pleas judge from 1945 to 1968. He knew what he was doing, and he was as aggressive as Egan. Indeed, when he retired from the Bench in 1924, he followed in Egan's footsteps as a lawyer who avoided the milk of human kindness as if it was undiluted poison. He gave nothing away at the Stimmel preliminary hearing.

A police witness identified Stimmel. Doctor Hatcher, the ex-coroner, testified concerning his finding and disposition of the body of the murdered man. Doctor Wilford Taylor testified concerning his post-mortem examination and his opinion that the death was caused by gunshots. Nothing there to stir up controversy. The final witness was Harry Brush who put Stimmel at the feed store with another man shortly before the time of the murder. He claimed that he saw both men go into the alley next to the store and adjust handkerchiefs over their faces. He claimed that he saw them demand that Shide and Fishbach take them into the office. He claimed that he had known Stimmel for three years and knew Stimmel's voice as well as his appearance.

If Stimmel's eyes had been revolvers, Brush would have died on the witness stand at the preliminary hearing. The unwavering glare from Stimmel during Brush's testimony was matched by the unwavering credibility attacks of Egan's cross-examination. "Did Stimmel have a mustache on the night of the murder?" "Unequivocally, no." "Hadn't you and your friends been involved in a fight with Stimmel at Mike Dunlevey's saloon sometime before the murder?" "Yes, but…" "Hadn't you run with a gang of thieves in East Dayton?" Denied. "Hadn't you

Montgomery County Jail 1874–1965 on the north side
of Third Street between Main and Ludlow streets.

visited Seiler's place on Third Street and Mike Dunlevey's on the East End?"
"Well, yes." "Haven't you quarreled with Stimmel over a woman?" "Well, yes."

A preliminary hearing is not a setting for the resolution of credibility contests,
nor is a grand jury proceeding. Squire Terry bound Stimmel over for the state's
presentation to a grand jury. Prosecutor Martin's next move was to serve a grand
jury subpoena on Rose Shafor who was described in the press on October 15, 1903
as "the sister to the notorious Cook brothers, criminals and convicts." Guess who
represented Rose Shafor? You're right. It was Jack Egan. Guess what Rose did
when she got the subpoena? You're right. She refused to testify.

At that point Judge Alvin Kumler, who would preside over the Stimmel trial, entered the scene. Rose was cited for contempt of court for her refusal to testify and placed in jail where she would remain until she agreed to purge herself of contempt by providing her testimony. She did remain in jail in silence until after Stimmel was convicted on Christmas Eve.

The words that finally emerged from Rose's mouth after her lengthy incarceration for contempt became the subject of a sub-headline in half-inch print in the *Dayton Daily News* just below an announcement in one-inch print that "Death In Electric Chair Is The Doom That Now Awaits Charles Stimmel." The sub-headline read as follows:

'They have convicted an innocent man.' This is the utterance of Rosa Shafor after her release from the city jail immediately following the verdict, but her words are meaningless for the reason that her voice was never raised in court on behalf of the man for whom she abandoned home, honor and self-respect.

Previous references to poor Rose in the media had indicated that she had no home, honor or self-respect to abandon. Be that as it may, neither she nor Egan received any favors from Judge Kumler.

Kumler came to the Bar in 1875, and he became a Common Pleas judge in 1896. He was one of eight brothers who all entered into the legal profession. He died in 1905, a year after the death

Newspaper sketch of Judge Alvin Kumler.

of Charles Stimmel. Judge Kumler was not only outraged at Rose Shafor's refusal to testify. He was even more outraged at Egan's representation of her, the defendant and the defendant's mother. True, by today's standards, such a potential and apparent conflict of interest would not be condoned. The level of outrage in 1903 may be a little high, however, especially considering the fact that the judge's brother, Charles Kumler, served as assistant prosecutor with Ulysses Martin in the Stimmel trial. It is also worthy of modern comment that the whole story of the police investigation and the tracing of the actions of Stimmel and Shafor were published in detail in October of 1903 under headings which included "secrets from the room of the grand jury."

After Judge Kumler threw Rose in jail for contempt, and the sheriff refused to permit Egan to confer with her, Egan went to probate court with one of his famous writs of habeas corpus to obtain the right to confer with his client as her attorney. Probate Judge B. F. McCann granted the writ and confirmed the right of an imprisoned person to meet and consult with his or her attorney in private. The probate hearing on the writ produced considerable fireworks between Egan and Sheriff Wright, comments which on several occasions came to the verge of blows. Even after the court's ruling the sheriff protested the cloak of privacy to which the attorney-client conference was entitled. When Jack and Rose had their lengthy private conference, Sheriff Wright looked daggers at Jack and told him, "I've always treated you square, but I won't do so anymore." On the subject of fairness, Prosecutor Martin in the probate hearing attached to his legal memorandum a list of all the questions he intended to ask Rose in the grand jury—questions that poured poison into the defense of the case when published in the eagerly awaiting press.

Two days after Jack's success in probate court, he was ordered into Judge Kumler's court to show cause why he should not be cited for contempt for calling to Rose through the bars of her jail cell and warning her to make no statement to the grand jury—conduct that allegedly occurred when, prior to the probate court hearing, the sheriff had refused to permit Egan to have a private conference with Rose. The motion filed by the prosecutor and presented to the press offered the prosecutor's personal opinion that "I am satisfied that Rose Shafor knows who committed the murder, if she would tell the truth." Egan was charged in the motion with obstructing the administration of justice in Montgomery County.

There was definitely a lot of zeal expended and flying in both directions in the period leading up to the trial. Egan avoided joining his clients in jail, but—because of the alleged conflict of interest in representing multiple clients—Judge Kumler refused to appoint Egan to represent Stimmel at the trial. Instead he appointed as Stimmel's defense counsel a young attorney named Walter Hallanan plus Elihu Thompson who had been a Dayton lawyer since way back in 1862 and had served a short time on the Common Pleas Bench with Judge Kumler. Undeterred, Egan proceeded to shove aside the appointed counsel and to take over the defense as Stimmel's personal counsel. The stage, already drenched in rhetorical blood, was set for the drama that began on December 9.

Forty-two jurors were summoned when the trial began on a Wednesday. All counsel and the defendant were assembled. Annie Van Horn, Stimmel's mother, sat behind him. His father who was paying for his defense by Egan was not in the courtroom, but was noted as taking a great interest in the case. Judge Kumler was bothered by an accident to a ligament in his leg and was forced to use crutches to walk to his seat behind the bench. That may have affected the somewhat ill temper he displayed throughout the trial. Additional jurors had to be summoned. By Friday the eleventh the jury had been picked, and Martin opened the proceedings with a dramatic reading of the indictment which started the tears flowing down the cheeks of Stimmel's mother. He went on to describe the crime as the "least justifiable, most cowardly and the cruelest homicide ever recorded on the annals of crime in Montgomery County." He indicated that he would prove that after the crime Stimmel met Rose Shafor and her little boy, that they went east on Third Street drinking at several saloons, and ultimately took a traction car to Springfield. Then they vanished until Stimmel was apprehended in Denver. On his arrest Stimmel claimed he had never lived in Dayton, but was a native of Texas, the Lone Star State. The defendant's opening statement emphasized that a man cannot be convicted on suspicion, and it outlined the alibi that Stimmel was not even in the City of Dayton on the night of the murder.

The first State witness was called on Friday afternoon. He was a sheriff's deputy who presented and explained in detail a chart of the scene of the murder. At that point the jury was sequestered at the Algonquin Hotel for the duration of the trial. Saturday night the bailiff and sheriff took them to a comedy at the Victory Theatre starring Charley Grapewin who many years later would be featured in the film adaptation of "The Grapes of Wrath." On Sunday the jury was taken to church to hear a sermon on "manhood."

Everyone came to court Monday morning with the exception of Prosecutor Martin who had suffered some heart problems on Sunday which required a recess until Tuesday morning to permit some recovery. When the trial resumed on the eleventh, the State's case moved slowly forward with a series of "just the facts" law enforcement witnesses punctuated with heated exchanges of attorneys which prompted Judge Kumler to give periodic lectures on demeanor and periodic threats of contempt citations. His fierce glares were directed more often at Prosecutor Martin than at defense counsel. There was repeated testimony in an effort to persuade the jurors that street lights were burning in the vicinity of the store when the crime occurred. Cross-examination of the first officer on the scene attempted to turn light to darkness by pointing out that a lady was nearly run down by a switch engine coming across Wayne Avenue in the dark.

The police witnesses had encountered Harry Brush, but objections were sustained to the prosecutor's questions about what Brush allegedly told them at the scene. Most of the trial week was consumed with such testimony. On Friday afternoon Doctor Hatcher who was the county coroner at the time of the crime was called to the stand. Prosecutors still love to end a trial week with the blood and gore testimony. Doctor Hatcher described the bullet wounds, and Prosecutor Martin got into another heated exchange with defense counsel over leading questions and arguing his case in the guise of witness examination. At one point Judge Kumler threatened to adjourn the court if the lawyers refused to quit fighting in front of the jury, thereby eliciting a final growl from Martin who had the judge's brother lie on the courtroom floor as a living example on which the coroner could demonstrate the path of the bullets, using—of course—his finger instead of a revolver.

Cross-examination focused on when the sun went down on the night of the murder. Judge Kumler referenced the parties to an almanac to determine the setting of the sun and the rising of the moon. Martin said "call the man in the moon; he is the only competent witness." Judge Kumler's brother, the assistant prosecutor, added the observation that "the almanac has a picture of a lion stirring mud." Professional respect in the proceedings—like the court's quality of mercy—was more than a bit strained. Doctor Hatcher on cross-examination did testify that Harry Brush at the scene "was pale and seemed excited," a bit of useful information for the defense.

Court was back in session on Saturday the twelfth. Things again got out of control over the testimony of Thomas McMahon, a police officer who came to the feed store as soon as he heard of the shooting. He testified that he made a fruitless search for Charles Stimmel in a lumber yard where fugitives were supposed to have hidden. Objection to the implicit hearsay in this testimony that his search was specifically for Stimmel set off another round of acrimony with accusations of impropriety from defense counsel, growls from Martin, and threats of contempt citations from the judge. The explosions occurred again when McMahon said he had seen Stimmel in the area earlier in the afternoon of the crime. He claimed that he had been told that Stimmel was a bad man and that he might have to handle him roughly if he ever had occasion to arrest him. The explosion resulting from that hearsay left Judge Kumler threatening to adjourn court and postpone the trial indefinitely if the lawyers could not act like lawyers.

The rest of the day was spent with two more doctors going back over the autopsy findings and the secretary of the Board of Police Directors testifying again about street lights at the scene of the crime. It may be poor taste in discussing a murder trial to refer to all such testimony as beating a dead horse, but the trite expression seems applicable. Another explosion precipitated and exacerbated by Martin. Another heated lecture from Judge Kumler. Then the jurors were permitted to go back to their hotel for a Sunday of rest.

The next week of trial brought to the stand the witnesses on whom the prosecution's case would turn. The testimony began with witnesses who were designed to confirm that the electric light at the railroad near the feed store was burning bright on the night of the murder. The goal was to provide a cushion of credibility for Harry Brush who would be one of the prosecution's star witnesses. The witnesses were not permitted to repeat what Brush had told them, and the rest of their testimony was as mixed as the light and dark evidence. Warren Hall worked at the Stoddard Manufacturing Company, a half-block from the feed store. At sundown on the night of the murder he saw three men near the railroad track about 150 feet from the store. One was tall and wore a cutaway coat. One was shorter and wore a black sack coat. The third had a brown sack coat. The tall one was about the size of Stimmel, but on cross-examination Hall acknowledged that when he was taken to the jail to observe Stimmel he could not say that Stimmel was one of the men.

Frank McCain worked at the Home Telephone Company next door to the store. He testified that Harry Brush sometime between 6:00 p.m. and 8:00 p.m. on November 22 ran into his office to tell of the hold-up. The police were phoned, and McCain and Brush ran back to the store. McCain ran into the door and was stopped by a man with a revolver who told him to get out. He ran behind a building and saw two men come out of the feed store and run toward Third Street. He gave contradictory testimony as to whether he could identify either of the men as Stimmel, and on cross-examination he testified as to some curious behavior of Brush. He indicated that Brush did not follow him into the feed store but instead ran into a railroad watchman's shanty and took off his blouse. The blouse had not been seen since. McCain was so unnerved by his cross-examination that he was unable to return to the stand when he was recalled by the State on Tuesday afternoon.

William Eaton drove the patrol wagon which was the first to reach the feed store after the crime was reported. When he arrived, Officer Clayton got off the wagon to inspect the scene. Harry Brush jumped on the wagon and told him to drive to Third Street and they would catch the murderer. He did, and they didn't. On cross-examination he indicated that bloodhounds were brought to the scene and that they traced a trail to Baer's Roadhouse where a suspect named Cunningham was arrested. He acknowledged that fifteen different people were arrested on the night of November 22 on suspicion of having murdered Shide. All were released.

The State finally called to the stand William R. Fishbach who was acknowledged to be the only actual witness to the murder of Shide. He recited the story that had been told at the state's opening statement concerning the events of the murder. The only light in the office at the time of his encounter with the two masked men and the murder of Shide by the tall one was what came through the window from the arc light at the nearby railroad crossing. Later he saw Brush, McCain, officers, reporters and bloodhounds at the feed store. He acknowledged that he and Shide had been working at the elevator across the driveway from the store, that it was Harry Brush who beckoned them to come to the office, and that Brush disappeared after they left the elevator. He was aware of the publicity following the murder and the reward offered for information leading to the arrest of Stimmel. He was taken by the police after Stimmel was returned in custody from Denver nine months after the murder, and at that time and again at trial he identified Stimmel as the tall man who had killed his co-employee.

Fishbach was a nice young man who made a good impression on his direct examination. The credibility of his identification of the defendant was, however, somewhat dubious. He had seen in semi-darkness a masked man during an event that lasted only a short time under highly stressful and unanticipated conditions. How was he able nine months later to identify the defendant as that man? His answer burst the bubble of his credibility in the minds of many observers. He claimed that Stimmel's appearance came to him like a light. The moment he saw Stimmel a light shining in his mind told him that Stimmel was the tall man who had murdered Shide. "Was it a dream?" asked Egan. "No, a stern reality," interrupted Charlie Kumler.

As the cross-examination progressed, the testimony drifted farther and farther into dreamland. Fishbach said that these strange lights controlled his every action. Sometimes while he was walking along the street, revolving in his mind some matter about which he was undecided, lo, a great light would suddenly descend. And there would be light cast into his mind that would outline his thoughts. It would cause a strange vision to appear before him. One part of the pathway would be as black as night; the other half would be resplendent with a brilliant illumination.

The path of light would hold the figure of a man. In this man he recognized himself. He knew that by his figure walking in the path of light, that he was to follow the illuminated pathway and not proceed in the dark and gloomy way. He would at once cease "following wandering fires" and march along the path of light. Sometimes at night he would be walking homeward along a certain street. He did not give the names of any streets, but said he would be walking homeward and the light would dawn warningly, before him, spreading its rays in the way that he should go. He would retrace his steps and go home by another route. At night, he followed the light and said his entire actions were controlled by it.

After such testimony it was up to Harry Brush to carry the prosecution over the hurdle of reasonable doubt. Brush was another employee of the feed store. He testified that he had worked all day when the crime was committed. He had gotten back from a trip at three o'clock and remained at the store until the murder. He waited on some customers at 5:15 and followed the grocer's exchange wagon out of the driveway. When he returned he saw Stimmel, a man with whom he was well acquainted. Stimmel walked north on Wayne Avenue and turned east into an alley north of the store. Brush saw Stimmel join another man in the alley. At that point he summoned Shide and Fishbach into the store as he believed there would be a hold-up or robbery.

Looking through the office window he saw Stimmel and the other man tying handkerchiefs on their faces. He barred the door at the front of the store that faced Wayne Avenue. Then he saw Shide, Fishbach and the two masked men come through the side door into the store. At that point he exited by the front door just as Stimmel shot Shide in the leg. He ran to the nearby telephone company to summon help and call the police.

On cross-examination defense counsel attempted to transform Brush into the murderer of Shide. The first step was to underline his testimony that Stimmel did not have a mustache on the night of the murder. The next step was to lacerate Brush's character with the numerous different places he had lived, the saloons that he frequented, and the company that he kept. The next step was to highlight his behavior on the night of the murder—bringing the victims into the store, being conspicuously absent when the crime occurred, his side trip to the railroad shanty, the wild goose chase after the man who may have been himself or his accomplice. The last step was to suggest motivation—prior altercations with Stimmel involving bar fights and rivalry over a lady. Statements about "getting even with Stimmel," knowledge of the contents of the safe at the feed store, knowledge that Shide kept the day's income in his pocket until it was time to place it in the safe at the end of the business day. Denials don't erase suggestions.

The strength of the prosecution's case came from evidence of Stimmel's behavior following the event for which he was indicted. The State called both the motorman and the conductor of the Dayton, Springfield and Urbana traction car on which Stimmel and Rose went from Dayton to Springfield on the night of the murder. They testified that Stimmel and Rose were with another couple when they got onto the car, that they had a boy with them, that Stimmel was drunk, and that Stimmel, Rose and the boy got off the car in Springfield. Margaret Brooks of Harshman Road and her daughter were on the car. They testified that they had known Stimmel, Rose and Rose's son a long time and that the three had been living at the Cook's home on Harshman Road before the murder.

A deputy sheriff from Clark County testified that he recognized the defendant as the man who lived with a lady and boy in Springfield as Mr. and Mrs. Cook. Those three lived in Springfield for six weeks after moving there in October of 1902. The little boy played with his son and was in his house nearly every day. He didn't see Mr. Cook after the couple moved in, but he saw Mrs. Cook often until December of 1902 when she sold their furniture and moved away.

Detective McBride testified concerning his investigation, his trip to Denver in August of 1903, and his arrest of Stimmel. On cross-examination he acknowledged that he had taken a statement from Stimmel at police headquarters on their return from Denver. The statement which had been transcribed was read to the jury. It confirmed that Stimmel denied any involvement in the crime.

In the late afternoon of Friday, December 21 the State rested its case. Concern was expressed that the jury might be locked up in the jury room on Christmas Day. Judge Kumler told them that it is contrary to Ohio law in so serious a case to let

Newspaper sketch of Detective Frank McBride.

any jurors out of the surveillance of the court's bailiff. The jury would continue to either be in the courtroom, their jury room, or their hotel until their verdict was rendered. To add to the darkness of that prospect the defense called as its first witness the watchman at the railroad crossing on Wayne Avenue near the feed store. He was on duty the night of the murder and confirmed that the light at the crossing was not burning at the time the shot was fired or thereafter. That fact was confirmed by three other witnesses, a bystander, a railroad yard conductor, and a railroad yardmaster. The day ended with the jury well informed that the night of November 22, 1902, was a dark night. Nonetheless, Stimmel's behavior after that night still might make December 25, 1903 a dark day for him.

The jury went together to church on Sunday the twentieth and came back together to court on Monday the twenty-first to hear four separate defense witnesses testify that Harry Brush had said to them "if I had not shown Stimmel up, he would have shown me up." Six more witnesses testified that, based on experiments conducted at the store on December 15, 1903, it would have been too dark in the feed store at the time of the murder to identify anyone. Harry Clingman testified that he was the man who is said to have gotten onto the traction car drunk at the point where Stimmel, Rose and Rose's son boarded the car on the night of the murder. He also testified that Brush, after Brush had testified, told him in the corridor of the courthouse "go in and rap Slim (meaning Stimmel), but don't say anything against me." On cross-examination by the judge's brother he amplified Brush's comment to him as including "rap Slim and turn state's evidence."

Tuesday and Wednesday of the last week of trial featured a long parade of witnesses as to Stimmel's good character and the fact that he wore a mustache at the time of the incident and could not have been clean-shaven as described by Brush. There were also witnesses who remembered statements made by Brush which conflicted with Brush's trial testimony and implicated Brush as the probable murderer of Shide. One witness indicated that Brush had acknowledged taking money out of Shide's pocket after the murder, hiding it in his blouse, and then securing the blouse in the railroad watchman's shanty. There was testimony that during the time the crime was committed Stimmel was at his mother's home with Rose and her little boy and that later in the evening he was in a saloon among friends at a considerable distance from the crime scene. Stimmel's father testified on his behalf and produced a photograph showing Charles and Rose. He testified that the photograph was taken a few days before December 1, 1902. The photograph showed that Charles had a significant mustache that could not have grown in a week or two.

After the defense rested the State presented some rebuttal witnesses who testified as to the good character of Harry Brush. As might be expected, the closing arguments of counsel rattled the rafters of the 1884 courthouse. Jack Egan was reported as giving "an eloquent and magnificent speech, covering the entire case from its inception to its close." Looking back on the case and on Egan's skillful dismantling of the credibility of the two key witnesses for the State, it becomes tempting to conclude that a verdict of "not guilty" would have been within reason if Dayton Slim had not fled from Dayton to New Orleans and then to Denver after the crime was committed. At 7:30 on Christmas Eve, after a lengthy charge from Judge Kumler, the State's case against Stimmel was submitted to the jury.

The *Dayton Daily News* on December 25 reported that "death in the electric chair is the Christmas present Charles Stimmel received at 10:20 Christmas Eve." The sheriff held Christmas services in Stimmel's cell complete with scripture readings and a group of young men from the Y.M.C.A. who sang "Nearer My God To Thee." Jack Egan was not stirred by the holiday spirit. He continued the bitter fight on behalf of his client right up to the moment Stimmel drew his last breath.

Electrocution was set for April 19, 1904. Motions for a new trial and appeals were denied. Hearings were held before the Board of Pardons. There were several reprieves from the governor to permit further investigation including one reprieve that happened just as the prison officials opened the door of Stimmel's death row cell to take him to the chair. Egan pinned his last hope on the photograph taken of Stimmel close to the time of the murder that showed him with a mustache whereas the eyewitness at trial described him as clean shaven. The photographer's studio in Cincinnati was located at the eleventh hour, only to unearth the unfortunate fact that the photograph had been taken months before the murder. There was plenty of time between the date of the photograph and the date of the murder for a mustache to disappear. As the eleventh hour was passing Egan asked the Board if the sentence would be commuted to life if Stimmel identified the people who were involved with him in the fatal burglary. When the Board said "No," Egan's reply was, "Well then, he is innocent." It sounds sort of like a confession, doesn't it?

Innocent or not, Stimmel's last words as he sat without a tremor in the electric

Newspaper sketch of Jack Egan.

chair were a dying man's curse on the judge and prosecutor who sent him to his grave. I know one other Dayton lawyer who witnessed his client's last ride in the electric chair. It is a tough task after you have burned out all of your own wit, skill and energy in the effort to avoid that conclusion. I'm sure that Stimmel's electrocution was a tough moment for even as tough a person as Jack Egan. By the same token, Jack's extraordinary efforts on behalf of Stimmel had made his reputation as a great criminal defense lawyer.

Rose continued in her career after Stimmel's death, and her family and friends continued to provide plenty of business for Jack. The Cook gang morphed into the "Bungaloo" gang which was named after the building that was the gang's headquarters. The gang's crime sprees continued unabated until 1908, by which time Rose was serving a seven-year sentence in the Ohio Penitentiary on a charge of robbery and all the rest of her troops were sequestered in various prison cells. In 1907, the City of Dayton had announced that it had scheduled the Bungaloo Resort, a notorious school of criminals, to be razed.

SCENE 5:
Political Backrooms

In the second decade of the Twentieth Century the dyer's hand became colored as much by political corruption as by professional street crime and murder. Rodney J. Diegle was a sergeant-at-arms of the Ohio Senate. He was also the point person for carrying bribes to Ohio senators on pending legislation. Jack Egan was at his side through the judicial ordeals generated by that conduct. Diegle was ultimately convicted of complicity in legislative bribery and started serving a three-year sentence at the Ohio Penitentiary in September of 1911. His was the first trial resulting from twenty-seven indictments involving thirteen different defendants. Co-defendants in his indictment were state senators from Montgomery County, Butler County and Lawrence County. The charges against these co-defendants were severed for subsequent trials, and the case against Diegle went to trial in the first week of June of 1911. A guilty verdict was entered on July 8, 1911, after sixty-six and a half hours of deliberation.

Two aspects of the case are of special interest one hundred years later. To his credit Egan served exclusively as Diegle's attorney. Other attorneys in the case purported to represent all of the defendants and potential defendants in the bribery investigation and prosecution. The problems of loyalty, confidentiality and conflict of interest inherent in such representation would not be condoned today, and modern lawyers look back in amazement at an era when representation of multiple defendants was not uncommon. It was also an era where it was not unusual for a corporate lawyer to represent a corporation, its individual officers, its individual directors, its individual shareholders and their various family members while serving also as a member of the board of directors of the corporate client. There are indeed some advances in the law as time goes by.

The second feature of the case worthy of comment is Egan's effort to give birth to the defense of entrapment. His client was the designated goat or go-between engaged to facilitate bribes between lobbyists and state senators. The specific conduct framed by his indictment involved detectives who at the direction of prosecutors were posing as lobbyists. Jack argued that his client had been entrapped into criminal conduct, that he was acting as the agent of the detectives who were offering bribes, and that Diegle on principles of *respondeat superior* was guilty of no crime if those detectives were not guilty of any crime. If Diegle lost the case after a lengthy jury deliberation, it wasn't because his lawyer lacked ingenuity.

There was quite a publicity aftermath between the date of the verdict and September 15 when Diegle started serving his sentence. Was Diegle going to turn informant with a full confession that would jeopardize the liberty of all those senators who were trembling in the wings of the courthouse awaiting a commencement of their separate trials? Such an approach in Diegle's self-interest certainly appears to have been Jack's post-trial strategy. It only ran aground with an echo of what had happened when the Board of Pardons refused to cut any slack for Dayton Slim. After much discussion the prosecutors in the senate bribery cases refused to make any deal with Diegle. On September 15, 1911, Diegle made his written "confession." He "confessed" that he had done no wrong and that all of the remaining defendants were equally innocent of any crime.

SCENE 6:

Gambits of a Golden Tongue

Jack did not confine his interpersonal and oratorical skills to the courtroom. He became a popular speaker at public events and an active member of fraternal organizations. He was involved in the formation of the Dayton Aerie of Eagles in 1903, and he was busy giving speeches, eulogies and songs at that fraternal organization from that date forward. Judges Sprigg, Baggott and Budroe—as well as other Dayton judges and lawyers—were members of the club which met regularly at the Phillips House Hotel at Third and Main streets and sponsored many dances, cribbage tournaments, pool tournaments and other festivities.

Jack was never at a loss for an imaginative legal ploy or a caustic public remark. When the chairman of the local Democratic Party in 1915 defended a police court political appointment with a reference to the old aphorism that he couldn't be expected to make a silk purse out of a sow's ear, Egan wrote him a letter in which he congratulated him on doing an even greater thing than making a silk purse out of a sow's ear—"you've made a police court judge out of a horse's ass."

This book began with the minimalist eulogy accorded Jack Egan at his funeral in 1936. In March 1912, Jack was called upon to give the principal address at the annual memorial services of the Fraternal Order of Eagles in Cincinnati. His speech demonstrated that the flowers of rhetoric with which he had graced his law school commencement ceremony had not wilted and died:

> Human life is like a tiny rivulet that has its source on
> an inaccessible mountaintop. As it rushes down the
> mountainside, it becomes a boisterous stream that
> tears a channel through rocky gorges, leaps over
> frowning crags, passes through purifying sand and,
> finally, limpid and clear as crystal, joins the waters

of some river. Then begins for the mountain stream a tumultuous career that might be compared to the life of a young man who gets his first glimpse of the world with its sorrows and joys. Through the entire changes incident to currents carrying it here and there and river meeting river in angry clash and hurrying it along, the mountain stream always returning something of its purity passes out into the great sea to be at peace forever.

It was reported that few addresses delivered on similar occasions in recent years had made a deeper impression on an audience. Alas, neither the three words spoken at his funeral nor the two hundred pages scratched into this book some eighty years later can provide a eulogy to match Egan's own Irish eloquence.

His personal life in the first two decades of the twentieth century featured the social joys of horse racing and gambling and the bibulous companionship of his fellow barristers. His wife Nellie remained quiet and supportive in the background. In 1908 we find them returning home after several weeks at the resort at French Lick Springs in Indiana, a favorite haunt of his close pal Judge Baggott. In May 1912, he moved his offices from 112 East Third Street to the new Schwind Building at 27 South Ludlow Street which became the home of a number of Dayton's leading lawyers and law firms. On April 26, 1913, in the aftermath of the great Dayton flood his mother died of organic heart failure at age seventy. At the time she had been living at 1014 West Fourth Street in Dayton.

Jack remained involved in Dayton club life and at the fringes of its political life. He was part of the Dayton delegation which arrived at the national convention in Chicago to root for Taft as president in 1908. He presided at the annual frolic of Dayton's legal fraternity at Wellbrook Camp north of the city in June 1912. By 1914, he was admitted to the Dayton Lodge of Elks as well as the Eagles Aerie and a social club called the Hoop de Doos. His St. Patrick's Day speech that year at the Elks Lodge received newspaper coverage with photos of Jack along with Judges

Baggott, Sprigg and Budroe who all participated in the festivities. In 1916 he was in charge of the fireworks at a Fourth of July picnic at which the three hundred charges of Saint Joseph's Orphan Asylum had the time of their lives. In the summer of 1919, he and Nellie managed to find time for a trip to Europe with friends. It is clear that Jack had not been rendered a dull boy by all work and no play.

Yet it was work that kept his engine running. And it should not be concluded that all of his work was the representation of rascals, crooks, hoodlums and gangsters in criminal cases. He was an all-purpose lawyer with a busy docket of civil cases, domestic relations matters, and bankruptcy filings. A typical Egan bankruptcy filing in 1910, listed among his client's debts "$10 to saloons and other necessaries." What could be more necessary than a man's bar bill? Many of his filings in divorce matters are studded with colorful comments. For example, a hapless husband complained of being compelled to dodge a fusillade of skillets, pots, pans and other missiles plucked from the culinary department of a household that was totally devoid of idleness. Another husband had a wife "as Dutch as sauerkraut" who frequently beat him into insensibility, threatened him with poisoning and threw him out of their unhappy home. Domestic intranquility was never so artfully expressed.

Egan always had a full assortment of civil damage lawsuits in play. In 1902, we find him representing a plaintiff in a suit against two police officers for false arrest and false imprisonment. In 1906, he sued the city for negligence in not providing ample protection for pedestrians at the intersection of Third Street and the canal. Presumably Egan had a wet client. He filed two civil suits on the same day in 1910. One was for the death of the driver of a city garbage wagon who suffered a horrible death under the wheels of a Dayton Street Railway car. The other was on behalf of the widow and four children of a man who met his death when he, his truck, and a heavy box of tobacco went down the elevator shaft at Billman Brothers Leaf Tobacco Company in West Carrollton. He won a verdict on behalf of Lizzie Harries, "one of Dayton's best-known and most estimable women," in a bitterly fought 1913 trial of a suit filed against her by the Schaur Distilling Company on a claim that she conspired to force it to vacate some premises which it rented from her. The verdict was especially sweet since the distillery was represented by two of the most prestigious firms in Dayton—Gottschall, Turner & Carr and Allaman, Kennedy & Retter. His forays into the civil side of the court's docket are notable both for their abundance and for their variety.

Civil or criminal, Egan matched his eloquence with an imagination that was always in quest of a winning gambit. He regarded law books in the same manner that W.C. Fields regarded the Bible. When found on his deathbed with the good book in his hands, Fields was asked if he had finally gotten religion. "Nope," he replied, "just looking for loopholes." In 1906, prosecutor Nevin was trying to secure the extradition from Oklahoma of an Egan client who was charged with larceny and burglary in Ohio. Jack found a defect in the authority of the governor of Oklahoma and asserted that the governor was therefore incompetent to sign the request papers. In 1910, he defended a client charged with violation of the rear platform smoking regulations of a Dayton streetcar company. His argument was that, like his client, he had been smoking on the rear platforms of streetcars for many years and never knew there was any statute to prevent it. In March 1911, he sought a new trial for Peter Ogle who had been charged and convicted of living unlawfully with Carrie Allen. His motion was based on evidence that the jury was so confused by the court's charge that they smuggled a dictionary into the jury room.

Egan knew how to use the unwritten law of human behavior to solve legal problems which the law could not fairly resolve. In 1914, he represented Mrs. Myra Kratzer who during a bad moment with her boyfriend shot at him five times in Dayton's Union Train Station. Her ex-husband and her little daughter were living in Muncie, Indiana. After a chambers conference in which the lawyers and the judge discussed the topics of reconciliation, reunion, and remarriage, Mrs. Kratzer was sent back to Muncie with the suggestion that she might not wish to return to Dayton. On at least one occasion Egan had the opportunity to apply the unwritten law from behind the bench instead of in front of it. He was asked to serve as a temporary judge on the Dayton Municipal Court on a single day in 1915. That day went down in local legal history as Bastille Day. His only act was to give suspended sentences to forty-seven individuals who had failed to renew their vehicle licenses.

The writ of habeas corpus remained Egan's favorite ploy for snatching clients out of the jaws of justice. In 1918, he used it to persuade Judge Routzohn of the County Probate Court to release a client who had been sent to the workhouse for refusing to submit to fingerprinting after he was arrested in an investigation of a jewel theft. Egan claimed he would file an injunction suit in Common Pleas Court to enjoin the police from forcing his client to submit to the fingerprinting system. As you might expect, it was the first case of its kind. Egan's routine use of the writ of habeas corpus to pull his clients out of jails and workhouses finally got him cross-wise with his old friend Judge Sprigg. It had reached a point where courts were putting Jack's clients into the front door of the workhouse and Jack was immediately taking them out of the back door of the workhouse with ex parte writs. Judge Sprigg in denying a writ sent out a general letter indicating that habeas corpus writs could no longer be used to attain the liberty of prisoners sent to the Dayton workhouse without notifying local authorities.

Dayton City Workhouse 1874–1933 at the northwest corner of Sixth and Main streets.

59

While Jack's gambits covered every legal and social arena he entered, the center ring of his legal circus was, and always remained, the defense of individuals charged with criminal conduct.

SCENE 7:
More Murder and Mayhem

Charles Stimmel was not the only client represented by Egan who would have fit smoothly into an Elizabethan revenge tragedy. Earl Foutz was an expert safe-cracker who had practiced his trade in Dayton, Columbus, Cincinnati, Lima and Hamilton. Caught in the act, he had the good fortune to have Jack undertake his representation, make an eloquent plea on his behalf, and work out a plea deal that reduced a potentially lengthy sentence to one that would give him freedom while he was still in his thirties. As he was being led from the courtroom, Foutz saw the detective who had arrested him and—using an epithet too strong to grace these pages—promised to get even with the detective as soon as the prison term expired.

Despite losses that any criminal defense lawyer must expect to encounter, Egan was an effective courtroom lawyer. Here is one of the murder cases in which he obtained a "not guilty" verdict. His client in a 1909 trial was a railroad detective named Hamilton Curry. The victim was a farmer who had a hardscrabble farm bordered by railroad tracks. The prosecution's story as narrated by the victim's weeping widow and daughter was that, recognizing their poverty and need, the detective had given them permission to pick up fallen coal on the railroad right-of-way to warm the shack in which they lived. Sometime later the detective came on their property with a warrant to arrest them for the very act that he had authorized. When the farmer threatened to explain that grant of permission to the detective's superiors, the detective shot him, not once but twice, producing two wounds either of which would have been fatal.

The detective's story was understandably different. He simply was trying to serve an arrest warrant when the farmer grabbed it out of his hands, tore it in two, and then came after him with a corn knife. The shots were fired in self-defense. In a case like this the defense lawyer's primary problem is how to attack the credibility of the weeping wife and daughter. A spectrum of techniques is available from gentle insinuation to hammer and tongs. Jack took the harsh end of the spectrum. The ladies were lying, and they deserved to be attacked head-on. Their testimony had to be interrupted by the court on several occasions during cross-examination to permit them to stifle their sobs and regain their composure.

Under the circumstances Jack made the right choice. He had the benefit of a client who appeared to be a nice guy. The client was also simply trying to carry out the duties of his job. To further balance the scales of justice, the client's charming wife and lovely daughters hovered behind him throughout the trial with more than occasional anguished glances to the jury. The knowledge that self-defense, where arguably applicable, is the best way out of a tough case would be of great benefit to Louis Parker in a notable trial twenty-five years later.

Self-defense remains the criminal defense lawyer's best friend in a murder case. The next best friend is the prosecution's star witness who either falls apart on the witness stand or never makes it to the courthouse. Fannie Hagelganz was a wealthy woman who lived alone on a farm near Orient, Ohio. She was murdered on February 14, 1909. Her partially decomposed body was discovered in her home on March 5, 1909. Three years later Luella Roebuck, the daughter-in-law of a neighboring farmer named Edward McKinley, told law enforcement officials that she had overheard Edward, his brother David, and Henry Hagelganz describe how they had killed Fannie who was Henry's sister. On January 15, 1912, Henry confessed to the police chief in Circleville and in the presence of the Sheriff of Delaware County that he had hired the McKinleys to kill his sister and that he had paid them $825 in blood money for the deed.

It sounds like a simple solution—despite the passing of time—to a nasty little murder. On January 17, 1912, fifty-three witnesses, including Luella Roebuck, testified to a grand jury. A search was made for Luella's husband Alonzo, but he was missing. On January 22, 1912, Henry was indicted for first-degree murder. On January 23, he retained Jack Egan to defend him. At that point the simple case started to get complicated. On January 26, the prosecution brought a companion indictment against Edward McKinley who was being held in jail in Franklin County on a lunacy charge. A black convict who occupied a cell close to McKinley informed the Franklin County Sheriff's office that McKinley had confessed to him that McKinley was the one who killed Fannie and that he intended to escape conviction by feigning insanity. He also told his jailhouse confidante that he had escaped conviction on another charge a few years earlier by the same ploy.

David McKinley made a statement that he had nothing to do with the murder and that he couldn't say whether or not his brother was involved. He offered the theory that Henry and a farmhand named Frank Coltz committed the murder and that Henry paid Coltz some money to help in the deed and then leave town. Coltz had in fact disappeared after the murder took place in 1909. David McKinley told the prosecutor that "you can dig six feet deep over the whole of the Hagelganz farm and you won't find the body of Frank Coltz." While this put a different spin on the whodunit question, it didn't really detract from Henry's confession on the who-paid-to-have-it-done question.

It certainly looked like Jack would have his hands full. On January 27, the physicians who examined Edward McKinley declared him sane. At about the same time, however, Luella Roebuck, like her husband Alonzo and the farmhand Coltz, became a missing person. Was Henry's confession admissible? If retracted, was it credible? Where was Luella? Where was her husband? Where was the missing farmhand? Where was there any other evidence to corroborate Henry's confession or illustrate the crime? Egan kept the focus on unanswered questions rather than on the probable answers to them.

The three missing witnesses were never found. The indictment against Jack's client drifted into limbo. On June 7, 1912, Henry Hagelganz was released from jail without bond since the state was unable to go to trial without its material witness. It constitutes a victory in football if you obtain the winning score simply because your opponent fumbled the ball in his own end zone. Jack had another victory in his career of defending murder cases.

Another case just missed by millimeters becoming a murder case. Early in his career Egan defended William Cook who, with another man was driving a wagon load of stolen loot out of Springfield on their way to Dayton. When they were stopped by a Springfield police officer, Cook allegedly jumped out of the back of the wagon, placed a revolver against the officer's side, and fired twice. Somehow the bullets went through the officer's clothes without touching his flesh—a phenomenon described as "a Shylock glance." A running gun battle followed, and the wagon was traced to a person on Wayne Avenue in Dayton who had rented it to the duo a few days before the incident. The luck of the shots, coupled with Jack's silver tongue, resulted in a not guilty verdict on a charge of shooting with intent to kill.

In 1906, Jack defended Roy Fowler on a charge of premeditated murder. The trial took place in the courtroom of Judge Ulysses Martin. Jake Nevin was the prosecutor. The evidence presented from the State sounds pretty persuasive. Two eyewitnesses testified that they saw Fowler shoot and kill Mayme Hagerty at the intersection of Second and Harshman streets in Dayton. In fact, they testified that he shot her twice before walking away with a smoking revolver in his hand. There was also evidence that a few months earlier Fowler had assaulted the lady and attempted to cut her throat. Jack tried to turn capital murder into manslaughter with the help of the axiom that love conquers all.

Judge Martin was kind enough to permit Fowler's mother to remain in the courtroom during the trial even though she testified as a witness for the defense. A mother's tears are a powerful forensic weapon. There was no premeditation argued Jack. The shots occurred in an unfortunate lovers quarrel. Fowler was a married man who had deserted his wife and children in the West to pursue his romantic passion for the desirable Mayme. It was Mayme's refusal to marry him that led to the fatal shots. While combining sex and self-defense would work years later for Louis Parker, sex without self-defense was not enough to spring Roy Fowler. Like Dayton Slim, he spent his last night on earth in an uncomfortable seat in Ohio's electric chair.

A year later Egan represented Abner Cain on a charge of burglary and larceny. When arrested, Cain had in his possession a bill from a company in Chicago for a casket, a suit of clothes and embalming expenses. He also had in his possession a receipt for a diamond which had been turned over to "an attorney in Dayton." The rumor that the bill related to the handling of Roy Fowler's post-electrocution remains was put to rest, along with Mr. Fowler himself, by proof that the body had been sent from the death chamber to Union Station in Dayton and properly and permanently buried here. The identity of the Dayton attorney who got the diamond was not disclosed.

If love and sex failed to work as a defense for Roy Fowler, the time-honored defense of confusion did work for Bert Parcells who was represented by Egan in 1909 at a preliminary hearing on a charge of murdering James Flannery with a knife. The cutting that led to Flannery's death was mild compared to the cutting up of witnesses by Jack's cross-examinations. He established that at the time of the murder Parcells and a companion of his had consumed six or seven buckets of beer and three bottles of whiskey. There were a number of ladies present at the scene of the crime, one of whom during the drunken orgy that led to the death had knocked Parcells off his feet by throwing a lamp which struck him in the head.

Tears and conflicting testimony flew in every direction as Jack did his work. In his cross-examination of the State's star witness he established that she had been arrested four times and sent on three occasions to the workhouse for loitering and drunkenness. He also demonstrated the even more helpful fact that she had been the victim's sweetheart for several years before the murder. By the time the hearing was over, there was no credibility to carry the charge and no way any rational judge could determine who wielded the knife that struck the fatal blow.

Another masterpiece of confusion arose over a neighborhood fight about a line fence which went ballistic with clubs, brickbats and two revolvers that fortunately failed to fire. Three people were charged with assault with intent to kill. Jack's cross-examination lived up to his reputation for courtroom aggression, and one witness announced in open court that he did not want to be bulldozed by John Egan of Dayton. Apparently, the assault in the courtroom was more impressive than the assault that brought the defendants to the court room. As cases of murder and mayhem continued to come into Jack's pathway, his reputation continued to rise.

The post-conviction energy and persistence Jack had displayed after the conviction of Dayton Slim was demonstrated again in the case of Frank Kinney who was convicted in Cleveland and sentenced to be electrocuted on August 15, 1913. His offense was the murder of a retired sea captain named Ralph Byrnes. Kinney and his girlfriend Nellie Sullivan were claimed to be part of a gang of burglars which had caused a three-month reign of terror in Cleveland. Mrs. Byrnes identified Kinney as one of two men who shot and killed her husband when she and her husband returned home from church to find the men engaged in burglary. Captain Byrnes wrestled a revolver from one of the men, and there was an exchange of shots with the other man, resulting in a fatal wound in the Captain's head. Kinney had given a statement that admitted the burglary, but said that his revolver had accidentally discharged when Byrnes threw him to the floor in the course of their struggle. A manslaughter conviction would have been far preferable under this scenario to the conviction for first-degree murder which resulted from the widow's account of events.

After the verdict Kinney's girlfriend engaged Egan to come to the rescue. James Cox from Dayton had become Governor of Ohio, and he was not an enthusiastic supporter of the death penalty. On July 30, Jack obtained from Governor Cox a ninety-day stay of the scheduled execution. He later obtained a second reprieve until December 12. He secured a letter from the Mayor of Cleveland urging commutation of the sentence to life imprisonment, and he brought Kinney's sweetheart, Nellie Sullivan, to Cincinnati where she swore she would do all in her power to find Kid Dugan, the second burglar and the man Sullivan now claimed to be the actual murderer of the old sea captain. With the help of the Chicago underworld she raised $8,000 to secure Jack's efforts on her boyfriend's behalf. On November 15, a month before the execution date, Jack wrote to the prosecutor that Kid Dugan who held the key to Kinney's defense and two women in addition to Ms. Sullivan were ready to present evidence which would corroborate Kinney's statement that

65

his revolver went off accidentally—a slightly different scenario from the "brutal murder" by Dugan which was the claim made by Ms. Sullivan.

As in Egan's post-conviction efforts on behalf of Dayton Slim, it proved impossible for Jack to turn promises into performance. A letter mailed from Cincinnati in what appeared to be a woman's handwriting was sent to Governor Cox. It read, "I am the Kid. I know who killed Captain Byrnes. I will tell everything when the time comes. I can't live long. I am dying of consumption." It was apparently placed in the "nice try" file at the Governor's office. The Governor sent word to Kinney to prepare himself for death. The electrocution of Frank Kinney was the first electrocution since James Cox became the state's chief executive. It was also the first execution presided over by Warden Thomas, the father of a young man who grew up within the walls of the Ohio State Penitentiary, enjoyed life at the Ohio State University in the Roaring Twenties, and became a beloved Dayton judge.

It is tough to be a criminal defense lawyer, even if you're as good as Jack Egan. Facts have a way of derailing desired results. Emily Dickinson in a noted poem described hope as "a thing with feathers." Well, a chicken is also a thing with feathers. And, as far as hope is concerned, you will find chicken on the menu of almost every restaurant in America. The hopes of criminal defendants are often no better than whatever hopes fill the small heads of such feathered food.

SCENE 8:
The Spectrum of Courtroom Spectacles

In the first two decades of his career Jack Egan had rubbed elbows with rascals at all levels of society, and he had displayed the same zeal, ingenuity and eloquence no matter what strata of society produced his client of the day. He was a true old-fashioned case lawyer, and anything that came in his door was grist for his mill. The inhabitants of Cockroach Castle were no different from the playboys of the western world. We have encountered a number of the former citizens. Here are a couple of the latter who needed Jack's help.

Hugh C. McClelland was a popular young Dayton dentist who lived in style with his wife and children at 207 W. Monument Avenue. He was a member of prestigious local men's clubs, a prominent supporter of gymnastics, and a feature of national bowling tournaments as president of the United Bowling Association. Not the kind of man to be caught stealing automobile tires. On a September night in 1913, however, two Dayton police detectives were summoned to the home of J. G. Schenck at 228 N. Ludlow Street on a complaint that tires had been stolen from the owner's parked car. They found the tires hidden under a nearby voting booth, and thereby hid themselves in the area to see if the thief would return to recover his loot. The answer to your anticipated question concerning the presence of a voting booth on Ludlow Street in September of 1913 is, unfortunately, lost in the mists of history.

At one o'clock in the morning an automobile drove up Ludlow Street, veered to shine its headlights in a direction that illuminated the area under the voting booth, continued up Ludlow Street, turned around the corner, and then returned to the scene. Two men got out of the car, and the detectives jumped into action. Dr. McClelland was arrested at the scene. The other man—a teamster named Dusty Miller who worked at a Dayton ice plant—was arrested a short time later. On his arrest Dusty told the police, "Well, I am a poor guy and I suppose you will arrest me and let Dr. McClelland go." On his arrest Dr. McClelland called Jack Egan who announced that he would represent both defendants and that, when the facts in the case were learned, both defendants would be cleared. Dusty's prognostication proved only half true. He had apparently forgotten the concept of honor among thieves, and he was apparently ignorant of Jack's disdain for the niceties of legal conflicts of interest. The tires remained on the property of their owner where they belonged, and the defendants were able to retain the innocent status of mere passers-by.

Whether or not Dr. McClelland was involved in the 1913 tire theft, his net worth and social status were far exceeded by those of Nicholas Walsh, Jr. who hired Egan in 1917 to obtain an exemption from the World War I draft. Nicholas was the son of a deceased millionaire distiller and was continuing his daddy's profitable business in Dayton. At age twenty-one in 1916, he had needed Jack's help after getting into a drunken fight at the Hotel Gibson in Cincinnati and trying to escape arrest in a touring car he was too full of alcohol to operate. The police who had been required to use a blackjack to bring him under control were impressed at his fighting skills and reported him to be a physical marvel for his age. Egan was more successful on the disorderly conduct charge than he was a year later in arguing that Walsh's fallen arches rendered him unfit to fight for Uncle Sam and that selling whiskey in Dayton was a business commitment which could not be entrusted to anyone else.

Lack of success in legal proceedings, however, does not always generate an unhappy ending. Walsh was drafted into the Army, but he never entered the mud, blood and bullets that were features on the fields of France. He was stationed at Fort Morgan in Alabama where the fishing was good and where it was reported that he spread the gospel of good cheer and did more than anyone else in camp to keep the men in high spirits. His penchant for mischief and his personal fortune which was estimated at fifteen million dollars also made him a perfect client capable of paying his legal bills. Among other exploits, Walsh got himself sued for alienating the affections of the wife of the proprietor of a billiard hall in Chattanooga, Tennessee. He was also arrested in Cincinnati and charged with assault with intent to kill a cabdriver who had the temerity to charge $18 for a cab ride. Matching monkey business with real business, he expanded his pre-prohibition liquor business into a Dayton automobile dealership.

Walsh also continued to prove himself the dream client, a playboy in constant trouble with a constant source of the wherewithal to pay legal fees. In 1925 he became the defendant in the most sensational suit for divorce in Dayton history. The newspapers seized on it as the community's version of Hollywood Babylon, and the spectators at the trial were so numerous that the case had to be moved from Judge Baggott's domain in the 1850 courthouse to Judge Patterson's commodious courtroom in the "new" courthouse of 1884. When the trial session adjourned early on one of its multiple trial days, Judge Baggott expressed his sympathy to all the ladies of Dayton who would have to go home and attend to their housework.

Wild parties, nude pictures, letters disclosing the plaintiff's desire to raid the millions in the estate of the defendant's father, drinking binges, personal assaults. It was all there to entertain and titillate an audience which lacked the modern benefits of television soap operas and "reality" shows. The lady, who was obviously no "lady" in the Victorian sense of that term, claimed that she was Mr. Walsh's common-law wife and thereby possessed of the legal right to obtain a divorce. Jack Egan clearly recognized the distinction between saving damsels from distress and providing distress to damsels. He dished out a considerable amount of distress to the plaintiff in the Walsh divorce case. During his examination she collapsed on the witness stand on three separate occasions, each requiring a pause in the proceedings to permit her to pick up the pieces and regain her composure. Neither she nor the evidence presented a pretty picture, although both she and the evidence gave the spectators the spectacle they came to see.

Common law marriage has gone out of style and legal sanction. I still remember a client who had lived with her boyfriend as man and wife for over seven years in the good old days. She came to the office in tears, fixated on her desire to have a nice wedding and on her common-law husband's disinclination to incur the expense of such a superfluous ceremony. A lawyer letter to the reluctant common-law husband suggesting that his wife was ready to sue him for divorce if he did not say "I do" in a church in front of an admiring congregation produced a happy client with a dream come true. To my knowledge, the couple's marital bliss still continues. The legal criteria for a common-law marriage were not as clear in the Walsh divorce case, and the ending was not a happy one from the plaintiff's perspective.

At the close of the proceedings Judge Baggott read a seventeen-page decision which sent the plaintiff reeling in tears out of the courtroom with a conclusion of "no marriage, no divorce, no alimony." In summarizing the evidence which justified that conclusion Judge Baggott did not hesitate to cast a plague on both houses:

> During the term of the relationship there was an
> incessant recurrence of all sorts of abandonment,
> a more or less sustained carnival of debauchery

and lechery, reaching all degrees of unrestrained license, malicious destruction of property, a Saturnalia of shame, in fact every form of vicious pleasure, with the accompaniment of orgies and degradation, unrestrained drunkenness and riotous fighting with concomitant public odium.

It is apparent that Jack Egan was not the only possessor of both a law degree and a penchant for oratory in the city of Dayton. The Judge concluded by characterizing the parties in the following terms:

By their iniquitous, detestable and wicked conduct they became a pestilence and a curse in every decent community wherein circumstances created their licentious abode.

Even those housewives who had enjoyed vicarious pleasure as spectators at the courtroom drama were probably somewhat shamed and embarrassed by those remarks. Jack and his client, I suspect, were beyond embarrassment. The end, as always, justified the means, and Jack certainly had no trouble giving support to rich and nefarious clients.

Money isn't everything. Proof that no client was too humble to receive the full support of Egan's forensic skills is found in a scene from Cockroach Castle in 1914. Little Frank Behrle was a newsboy who peddled his wares in the vicinity of Union Station and placed his papers on the sidewalk in front of the depot while hailing prospective purchasers. Apparently some wealthy traveler tripped over the stacked newspapers, and little Frank was charged with obstructing the sidewalk. Jake Nevin was the prosecutor; Jack Egan represented the poor little defendant; and the two old cronies generated so much mutual vituperation at the trial that Judge Budroe threatened to send both of them to jail for contempt of court. Happily the boy caught in the middle of the heated exchanges did not go to jail. The learned judge ruled that he had the right to put his papers on the sidewalk while he pursued his legitimate business activity.

Years after Jack's death Herb Eikenberry, another colorful lawyer in Dayton, was asked from the bench by Judge Thomas to give an opinion on the reasonable value of attorney fees in a major criminal case where the pompous expert on the stand had testified that he only represented "good" criminal defendants. The lawyer called upon by the court to supplement the record professed that he was equally unqualified to opine on the appropriate fees in major cases since he only represented clothesline thieves and chicken rustlers. He may have been thinking of Jack's representation in 1914 of two men who were caught on a farm in Beavercreek shooting chickens, pulling off their heads, and stuffing them in a sack. The men escaped on a motorcycle when the farmer caught them in the act, but they left behind the telltale sack containing five dead chickens. I expect that Jack's defense was that beheading chickens is not a crime under the Ohio Revised Code and that, since no chickens were removed from the farm, there was no completed theft.

The first two decades of Jack's legal career ended with a client who was at the upper end of the spectrum of crime. He was a stark contrast to newsboys and chicken thieves. In April 1919, Jack represented Frederick Gondorf, the wiretapping King of New York, in a criminal case in the United States District Court in Covington, Kentucky. The charge was swindling a wealthy gentleman in connection with betting on racehorses in a first-past-the-post-game. If you have seen the movie *The Sting* in which Paul Newman played Gondorf or if you have read a book called *The Big Con*, you are familiar with the elaborate

Newspaper sketch of Fred Gondorf.

71

ways in which the Gondorf brothers and other notorious confidence men designed and executed schemes to extract huge sums of money from wealthy gamblers and investors who were looking for the "sure thing." The games have changed since 1919, but those who win and those who lose such games continue to recur with alarming regularity. W. C. Fields spoke the truth when he said "you can't cheat an honest man," but Mae West was equally truthful when she sang "a good man is hard to find."

The wiretapping game flourished in the pre-television and radio days when bookie joints received the results of horse races on the Western Union wire. Bets were placed; a race was then underway at a distant racetrack; the results of the race would come over the wire; money would be won or lost according to the odds and the results of the race. The con was based on the sting that Gondorf set up with the aid of an inside associate at Western Union who could hold the results of a race long enough to telephone the outcome to Gondorf in time for a "sure thing" bet to be placed by the confidence man's "mark." The amount the mark would put into play would be maximized by the drama of some big winnings in a few preliminary races.

The Gondorf brothers became legends in the annals of big time New York crime. They were reported to make one million dollars a year through wiretapping. George Gondorf had spent 1878 to 1883 in a Rhode Island prison for burglary, but avoided any convictions thereafter. Charlie Gondorf was sent to Sing Sing in 1918. After serving a four-year sentence, he left the prison in a big limousine driven by a liveried chauffeur and went to Europe to live on his income. Jack Egan was unable to obtain a favorable jury verdict for the third brother, Fred, in the 1919 trial in Covington, and Fred was sentenced to a five-year term in the federal penitentiary in Atlanta. At a 1924 United States Senate subcommittee hearing investigating misconduct in the Department of Justice, a senator expressed surprise that a big time con man from New York had been represented by an attorney from Dayton, Ohio. The explanation was that the trial did not take place in New York, but rather in northern Kentucky right across the river from Cincinnati.

Jack Egan was not unfamiliar with confidence men. There was a notable trio of such artists who chose the Opera Cigar Store on South Ludlow Street in Dayton as their venue for fleecing farmers in one of the greatest hold-up games ever practiced in this vicinity. When arrested, their first request was for an opportunity to call Jack Egan. But such clients were street corner guitar players compared to the master conductor of the New York Symphony in the person of Fred Gondorf. Jack's illustrious confidence man client served only two years of his five-year prison term, and part of the 1924 Senate investigation involved an alleged payment of $25,000 to a Washington attorney who knew the Daugherty gang and obtained executive clemency for Fred Gondorf. As students of Teapot Dome and the activities of Attorney General Harry M. Daugherty during the Warren Harding administration are aware, Harry came to Washington from Washington Courthouse, Ohio. He and Egan were not without professional interrelationships. The testimony before the 1924 Senate subcommittee did not implicate Jack Egan in the alleged bribe that reduced his client's prison sentence, but it does corroborate Jack's distinction of serving as trial counsel to one of the country's most notorious and most sophisticated criminals in the golden days following World War I.

Whether or not Jack Egan played an active role in securing Gondorf's early release from prison, it is established that he did play such a role in the early release of William F. Silva, the owner of the Newport, Kentucky gambling hall in which the Big Con was played. On April 12, 1919, Silva, like Gondorf, was sentenced to five years in the Atlanta penitentiary in connection with the Gondorf confidence game. He told a prison guard that he would give $100,000 to get out of prison. No information exists as to what, if anything, he paid to attorneys or anyone else to achieve that goal. Egan acknowledged, however, that he was engaged by Silva to try to obtain an early release and that, in turn, he asked his old crony Jake Nevin to assist him in that task. Nevin was prominent in Republican politics, having attended every Republican national convention since 1892. He was reported to be a close friend of President Warren Harding, and he acknowledged that he was engaged by Egan to seek a pardon for Silva.

There is nothing improper or dishonorable in such a legal undertaking, and the news reporters were quick to point out that "Nevin is known as a lawyer not identified with the sort of practice for which Egan is known." The two lawyers approached the prosecutor in Silva's case to seek his recommendation for Silva's pardon. The prosecutor wrote a letter indicating that he would concur in whatever decision was made by Judge Cochran who tried the case, with the proviso that all of the convicted defendants should be treated alike. Other support letters were solicited and received, including one from Judge Cochran who acknowledged that he was "a bit too severe" in his sentence and that Silva and his associates might have been freed if the search warrant law, as currently applied, had been applicable at the time of their trial.

On May 10, 1923, President Harding commuted Silva's prison sentence to expire in July of that year instead of its designated date in April 1924. While Nevin and Egan happened to be in Washington when that action was taken and despite the shadows of corruption that cloud the Harding administration and color every corner of Egan's career, there is no evidence of any tainted transaction impacting the reduction of Silva's sentence.

Egan's first twenty years at the Bar had fed his ambition and provided him with all the tools he would need to flourish in a world in which a whole new breed of outlaws and gangster clients were about to flourish. In accord with Macbeth's self-description, he surged forward into whatever fate had in store for him.

> The mind I sway by and the heart I bear
> Shall never sag with doubt, nor shake with fear.

Jack Egan was ready for the new clients a new decade would bring to him. I suspect that he was totally unaware of the fact that he had only sixteen years left to race with the burning chariot of his ambition and reputation across the sky above the land of the fee and the home of the grave.

ACT IV

Schwind Building on South Ludlow Street with Egan's office window.

Roaring Through the Twenties

1920 was a big year, especially in southwestern Ohio where James Cox, the Dayton newspaper boss who became Ohio's governor, was running as the Democratic candidate for the presidency of the United States with Franklin D. Roosevelt as his vice-presidential running mate. Cox had grown to manhood not far from Excello, and Jack had known him for years. The two men despised each other. When Cox announced that he had gone to his mother's grave for the inspiration to become a presidential candidate, Jack remarked that the only reason he chose his mother's grave was that he didn't know where his father was. Caustic comments aside, the decade of the 1920s was the golden age of Jack Egan's practice.

SCENE 1:
Games People Play

To the surprise of all who knew him—to say nothing of all who know of him from the stories that continued to be told and retold after his death—Jack Egan's opening act in the drama of the 1920s was as assistant prosecutor in a probe by Judge Budroe into gambling activities in Dayton. It was no secret that Jack himself was a gambler of note and that he was the lawyer sought by Dayton gamblers on those rare occasions when the law interrupted their games.

In April of 1909, gambling raids had been conducted at John Koors' place on Court Street near the Union Station and at the Monarch Club at 11 West Fourth Street. Fifteen men were arrested and sent to the central police station in the patrol wagon. John Koors, who later served the last free lunch in Dayton behind the famous swinging doors of Koors 29 on the north side of Fifth Street between Main and Ludlow streets, furnished bail for all fifteen defendants. Jack Egan, with his usual disdain for conflict issues, represented all fifteen of them.

In April of 1912, there was another gambling raid at the club rooms conducted by Gus Sigrib at 111 South St. Clair Street. Jack not only represented all eight men who were arrested in the raid; he demanded a jury and promised that there would be plenty of fire and excitement if the case came to trial. His promise included an expressed intent to issue witness subpoenas for Mayor Phillips, Safety Director Dodds, members of the police department and other city officials. He claimed that it would enliven the proceedings when such witnesses were required to tell their stories to judge and jury. Apparently the fire was never ignited; the stories were never told; and there were no proceedings to be enlivened.

Then came January 1920, the same month the noble experiment of Prohibition became effective. Frank J. Heck, the alleged head of the Fraternal Order of Oaks, was arrested on charges of having conducted a gambling establishment. He was represented by Carroll Sprigg and Al Dwyer who both withdrew from the case after Judge Budroe on January 19, turned it into a full-scale probe of gambling in Dayton and appointed a committee of attorney Earl H. Turner, Rev. Miles H. Kumbine and William Nunan to investigate the subject. The trial testimony certainly opened a window on a thriving—if illegal—Dayton activity. The average bets at the Oaks Club on horse races, stud poker, and dice games were upwards of $4,000 a day. The club was located on the second floor of the Pryor Building on Ludlow Street, near Fifth Street. There were ten to fifty men in the place every afternoon. The crap games started every night after midnight and lasted as long as a day and a night. Around $12,000 would exchange hands in those games, and nobody even stopped to eat.

Egan's participation as prosecutor was, to put it mildly, somewhat out of character. He acknowledged that he had drawn up the lease for the rooms in which the Oaks Club was conducting its gambling operations, and the testimony of the witnesses called established that Egan was the largest bettor among the regulars at the Club. His bets were typically in the $500-$600 range, and he was the largest bettor on horse races. There were at least five or six other gambling halls in Dayton, including a room in the Pryor Building run by Gus Sigrib. W. T. Tinnerman, the proprietor of the Pony House on South Jefferson Street, testified that the largest amount he had ever lost at one time at the Oaks Club was in the range of $2,000.

Judge Budroe took a very active and aggressive role in the proceedings, interrupting the testimony of an employee of the Club to call him a liar and charging the Dayton Police Department with complicity in condoning the million-dollar gambling house while conducting occasional raids on private homes where there were little penny-ante poker games being conducted by husbands and wives, while children played on the floor. At the end of the trial Judge Budroe explained his action in causing the investigation as having been forced on him by humiliation beyond the power of expression. The ultimate scapegoat was City Safety Director Harry P. James who was charged by Judge Budroe with protecting a larger gambling dump than he ever dreamed existed. A year later, on April 21, 1921, Judge Budroe died. Jack Egan gave a talk at his memorial gathering. It was noted that, when the final summons came, Judge Budroe went forward fearlessly and unafraid to meet the Greater Judge beyond.

In his closing statement at the gambling probe Jack asserted that the court had by necessity trailed the beast to his lair and exposed a diabolical business of which the police department had been blissfully unaware. If this spectacle appears to be nothing more than an appalling, hypocritical charade designed to find a public scapegoat for a continuing vice, do not be dismayed. Such spectacles have been and ever will be part of the American scene as long as greed, sex, drink, and gambling are among the mainsprings of the psyche of the American male—a span of time that seems unlikely to end.

Is it significant that this bizarre episode of Egan's participation as prosecutor in the Dayton gambling probe happened at the midpoint of his legal career? We will find that it did not turn him into a crusading Puritan or cause him to stray even an inch off his personal path to perdition. Nor did it serve to suppress gambling any more than the closing of bordellos in Dayton and elsewhere suppressed illicit sex. In fact, the suppression of the alleged vice of alcohol consumption in 1920 simply created a whole new congregation of clients in need of Jack's arts.

If he had lived another hundred years, I am sure that Jack would have been more amused than surprised at the proliferation of pornography that has resulted, at least in part, from the suppression of sex. And I am sure he would have the same reaction to a discovery that gambling has been taken over by state governments, in a second theft of livelihoods from Native Americans, as a technique for taxing the poor to support the rich. Nor would he be dismayed to find that the robber barons and confidence men of the late nineteenth and early twentieth century have been cloned as the new robber barons and confidence men of the late twentieth and early twenty-first century.

Was Jack simply a rascal? I would like to think better of him as a man who, as a result of his professional association with the riff-raff of Cockroach Castle and with the full spectrum of lawless behavior, developed an uncritical view of and appreciation for human nature in all its flaws and frailties. On the bright side, like Prince Hal in his youth, he happily inhabited a Falstaffian world of drunkards, thieves, prostitutes and cutthroats. Why didn't he emerge as Henry V? Do time, circumstance and opportunity provide an answer?

On the dark side, why didn't Macbeth and his lovely wife put their misdeed with King Duncan behind themselves and live happily ever after as King and Queen of Scotland? Why did Macbeth have to descend into the assassination of his friend Banquo and the cruel slaughter of Macduff's innocent babies? Perhaps Andrew Marvell had the answer in his *Horation Ode Upon Cromwell's Return From Ireland*: "the same arts that did gain a power must it maintain." Like Macbeth and Cromwell, Egan had set himself upon a path on which his nature compelled him to remain. The means would always remain secondary to the end.

Cogitate, meditate and figure it all out for yourself. My task as a humble local historian and biographer of a sometimes less than laudable lawyer is simply to report the facts and occasionally note the ironies. While I would like to confect a final elegance, my role is not to crusade, console, or sanctify, but plainly to propound.

SCENE 2:
Egan's Office — Inhabitants and Visitors

Jack Egan's office since 1912 was in the Schwind Building on the east side of Ludlow Street, near Fourth Street. What an office it was! Irving Delscamp had been an associate lawyer in Jack's office as far back as 1911, when the defense of Rodney Diegle was getting statewide publicity. It is said that Delscamp always brought his lunch to work in a brown paper bag since he wanted to be there when the mail was opened to make sure that he got his share of any fees the postman delivered. It was also said that when he was trying a criminal case, the client had to show up each morning with the fee for the day if he expected his lawyer to go to court with him, a practice that would generate disciplinary sanctions in the next century. While he stayed under Egan's shadow until Egan's death in 1936, Delscamp remained on the Dayton legal scene until his own death in 1973.

Delscamp was not the first lawyer in history to display an inordinate concern about his fees. Romeo's sidekick in his Queen Mab speech portrays all lawyers as "dreaming on fees." And Egan was neither the first nor the last criminal defense lawyer who inspired an inordinate public concern about the source of his fees. We shall see that issue bubble up later in connection with his representation of John Dillinger. It became a public issue as early as September 1923, in connection with the confession of a client represented by William Pickrel. Pickrel was a distinguished founder of a Dayton law firm that still bears his name. His client was a man named Fred W. Hecht.

Hecht was vice president and cashier of the American National Bank and Trust Company, a Dayton institution Mr. Hecht put out of business by converting over five years some $300,000 of the funds it held on behalf of depositors. In that Teapot Dome and Prohibition atmosphere, he had been infected with the investor's gambling fever and had lost the money by financial forays into western oil fields and into business enterprises designed to bypass the Volstead Act. He confessed that he had given $35,000 of the tainted money to Jack Egan to use in obtaining bonds to secure the release of arrested bootleggers.

There was a song which attained a modest level of popularity during that lively period of American history. It is entitled "How Could Red Riding Hood Have Been So Very Good and Still Kept the Wolf from Her Door." The best lines of the song run as follows: "Mother and father she had none, so where in the hell did all that money come from? I've got to ask it. Who filled her basket? The storybooks never tell." While no one could confuse Jack Egan with Little Red Riding Hood, the Dayton newspapers posed the same question in an article that featured a photograph of our favorite lawyer. Jack was in Chicago at the time, but he acted promptly and with his usual aggression in providing an explanation to the media.

That wasn't bond money held in trust for bootleggers. It was a fee paid by Mr. Hecht to Jack from Hecht's honest wages. It was reasonable payment for professional services rendered some years ago when Jack represented Mr. Hecht on a legal matter which the attorney-client privilege requires Jack to hold in confidence. It can only be disclosed that Mr. Egan had rendered capable and competent professional services and that what those undisclosed services accomplished was of great value to Mr. Hecht. Whether or not that explanation laid all public concerns to rest, it sufficed to keep the wolf from Jack's door. The inquiry was closed.

Other associates in Egan's office did not possess the staying power or conspiratorial character and compatibility of Irv Delscamp. 1927 brought a young lawyer named Wilbur Speidel into the office. After several years Wilbur worked up the courage to confront Jack and complain that he didn't think he was being paid what he was worth. "You are absolutely correct," said Jack, "and I'm going to provide you the opportunity to earn what you are worth. You're fired." Wilbur moved to

Greenville, Ohio where he became a lion of that small community's trial bar and, I suspect, succeeded in earning what he was worth over a long and successful career.

In 1922, a young lawyer named Calvin Crawford after graduating from Harvard Law School became an associate in the Egan law office. He was paid the princely sum of $15.00 a week to enhance his book smarts with street smarts. When Crawford lost the first series of cases he took to trial, Egan tried to improve his Harvard education with a little advice. "Now listen," said Egan, "don't let a little perjury stand between you and success. Go out and win a case." After a few years Crawford moved to more compatible pastimes. He ended up with a lengthy career as a common pleas judge and later, as an appellate judge.

Another short-lived associate at the Egan office was Charlie Brennan who didn't go to Harvard, but was nonetheless familiar with books. One day Egan found Brennan reading in the law library and asked him what he was doing. Brennan said he was reading so he would be ready if a client came in. Egan's reply was, "well, I'll just wait until someone comes in and then I'll get ready. I ain't being paid for what I already know." Brennan went on to become Mayor of Dayton and to enjoy a reputation as one of the most honest and ethical practioners at the Dayton Bar.

Another short-term associate in the Egan office was Albert Scharrer, a lawyer who was destined to replace Jack as Dayton's leading criminal defense lawyer. Scharrer practiced well into the 1960s, and I have vivid memories of seeing him in Court. He never forgot the pragmatic lessons he learned from Jack and from Charles Kumler, another criminal defense lawyer with whom he served an apprenticeship. Scharrer also garnished the additional benefit of viewing the practice of criminal law from the other table in the courtroom. In 1922, he became the Montgomery County Prosecutor and he served in that position until 1927.

In the same year of 1922, Roland McKee—later part of the triumvirate that ruled the notable Dayton law firm of Estabrook, Finn & McKee—ended his career as city prosecutor. That position passed to Lester Cecil who later became a municipal court judge, common pleas judge, federal district court judge, and chief judge of the United States Court of Appeals for the Sixth Circuit. Always an affable and popular member of the Dayton Bar, Jack Egan spoke at the ceremonial occasion which accompanied this change of position. He indicated that McKee had been such a good prosecutor that lawyers who frequented the court would be willing to give him almost anything to get rid of him. He added that if Lester Cecil is going to prove as efficient and untiring as the retiring prosecutor, the members of the bar would like to pay him not to accept the position before he takes office. Spoken in jest, those comments might carry a different tone in later years, in different circumstances, and with different individuals.

While he may have left law books to the likes of Charlie Brennan, Jack had a house full of literature and a retentive head full of classics that he could quote at length. With his quick wit and Irish charm and impressive appearance, he had the ability to capture a jury's attention and seduce or magnetize it to a desired result. If the facts or the law sometimes got in the way of a victory, there was never a loss for words on behalf of a Jack Egan defendant.

Sometimes Jack's clients were the victims rather than the beneficiaries of his ingenuity. The twenties were, of course, the wild days of Prohibition when booze flowed faster than it ever had in the days when it was a legal commodity. It is somewhat surprising that an underground alcohol pipeline was not installed from Chicago through Dayton to Hamilton. The overland route was nonetheless busy, and it was a rare day when our ambitious Macbeth did not entertain a bootlegger at his court on Ludlow Street. On one such day he had been dispensing legal advice to a Chicago bootlegger. When the bootlegger started to leave the office, he discovered that the car he had left in front of the office on Ludlow Street was gone.

Since the car was a special car fitted with numerous compartments full of bootleg whiskey, the client was more than a little concerned. Egan immediately brought the client back into the office, pulled down the blinds, and told him he thought he could recover the car, but the cost of getting it back would be $2,500. Relieved beyond measure, the client pulled the necessary money off a roll of bills and gave it to Egan. Warning the client not to leave the office or make any phone calls, Egan took the money and made a quick exit. A half hour later Egan was back, and the car was once again parked in front of the office. He gave the client the advice to get out of town as fast as possible, and the client promptly took that advice. Egan happily pocketed what was left of the $2,500 after the payment of the $10 improper parking and towing charge he had taken care of in his short absence from the office.

1927 was the first year in which Harry Jeffrey engaged in a civil trial practice that he pursued in Dayton until he reached the age of eighty-four. He never forgot the shock he received from Egan's cynical attitude toward clients in that first year of his long career at the Bar. As an idealistic young practitioner, Jeffrey had a client whose vehicle had sustained some minor damage in an accident. He wrote a letter to the driver of the other automobile demanding reimbursement for a $100 repair bill.

A few days later Jeffrey received a phone call from Egan who asked in his high-pitched voice that Jeffrey come to his office to discuss the case. Jeffrey complied. Upon his arrival at Egan's office he began his explanation of and justification for his client's modest demand. Egan interrupted him and said, "Look, the only thing my client has are two vacant lots, and they aren't worth much. I'll tell you what you do. You take one lot and I'll take the other." Shocked, Jeffrey asked, "What about my client?" "To hell with your client," replied Egan. "You take a lot." Jeffrey refused. He went back to his office, filed a Municipal Court lawsuit for $100 and obtained a default judgment in that amount against Egan's client. When he attempted to levy execution on the defendant's property, he found that both of the lots were in Jack Egan's name. Jeffrey never collected a dime.

Whatever may be said of Egan's unconcern for the niceties of professional ethics, his nose for a fee, and his slight regard for the clients who retained him or his adversaries, it is fair to say that he was somehow larger than life and that his main virtues and his main vices were essentially the same. He was completely non-judgmental in his views of human conduct and existence. He would undoubtedly have applauded the response of Pompey to Escalus in Shakespeare's *Measure for Measure*:

> How would you live, Pompey? By being a bawd?
> What do you think of the trade, Pompey? Is it a
> lawful trade?

If the law would allow it, sir.

But the law will not allow it, Pompey, nor shall it be
allowed in Vienna.

Does your worship mean to geld and splay all the
youth of the city?

We will leave to Shakespeare's great play the full exploration of the complexities of judging and being judged. Sometimes, however, in our professional reverence for the rule of law, we forget that it is simply a man-made structure for curtailing the wayward and wandering ways of ourselves and all the rest of our fellow citizens.

Jack relished his profane reputation, and that reputation was burnished with countless and oft-repeated stories. There is the story of Egan and one of his cronies engaged in an after-court drinking bout at a local tavern and getting into an argument as to whether Jack was so unredeemable a human being that he couldn't even recite the *Lord's Prayer*. Egan put his money on the bar, threw down another glass of whiskey, and slowly enunciated the following words:

Now I lay me down to sleep
I pray the Lord my soul to keep
If I should die before I wake
I pray the Lord my soul to take

"Well, I'll be damned," said his amazed drinking companion as he handed over the gambler's prize to Egan. "I didn't think you could do it."

The *Lord's Prayer* anecdote triggers a meditative pause in the pages of this narrative. It is an accurate reflection of the reality of Jack Egan's personality, but is it an accurate reflection of a real moment in time? If not, is its inclusion a flaw in this biography? I submit that the goal of biography is not the simple summoning of a dead individual from the darkness of the underworld. Its goal, or at least one significant goal, is the stimulation of the reader to examine his or her own values, beliefs, vices, virtues, character and personality in the distorting funhouse mirror of another's life. To the extent the other's life is admirable or appalling, that goal is furthered.

Most of the pages of this book are firmly grounded in contemporary documents and sources. The *Lord's Prayer* story may be an example of an observation that in the course of three generations of oral history facts morph into fictions. Remember the clever analysis of Ronald Reagan's political speeches that demonstrated the fact that most of his "personal experiences" turned out to be verbatim selections of scenes from old movies in which he had acted in his Hollywood days? It is difficult to prevent imagination from adding color to the black and white sources of memory. And where there is a choice between fact and myth, there is a strong temptation to print the myth. It is impossible to resurrect the dead with unblemished accuracy. It is, I suggest, more valuable to stimulate the self-awareness of the living.

In any event, there are more than enough substantial and fully documented events from the life of Jack Egan to ensure the accuracy of the portrayal of that life in these pages. Like many of the trial lawyers of his day Jack would occasionally disappear on legendary benders. He never, however, mixed work and alcohol. He was one of those men for whom one drink was too many and a hundred drinks were not enough. He knew he had to keep a steady hand to guide his clients through the mazes they and the law had created for them. Irv Delscamp, on the other hand, liked to take a little nip now and then during working hours, and he would sometimes get high in the office with the firm's bootlegging clients. Jack would get mad at this behavior since he was constitutionally unable to participate in it.

There was, of course, excitement in the world of bootleggers and outlaws who had become much more organized and professional than the gangs that existed at the turn of the century. Sometimes the excitement got a little too much even for Jack. One afternoon he offered a ride in his chauffeur-driven car to the son of a local lawyer. As the young man climbed into the car, another car pulled up alongside it on Ludlow Street and the occupant of that car discharged a machine gun at it. Despite the protective presence of bullet-proof glass, the passenger never accepted any more rides from Jack. As the decade lurched toward its close, Jack developed an understandable concern for his own safety.

SCENE 3:
Lethargic Law and Dynamic Disorder

A friend of mine has a son who was an impressive offensive tackle in his college days as a Big Ten football player. He also spent several years with the Atlanta Falcons until injuries took him out of the NFL. After his first day at the Falcons training camp, he called his father and said, "Dad, this isn't a game anymore; this is serious business and these are real men who are deadly serious about getting a position on the team." The days of once more into the breach with a band of brothers with whom it is all for one and one for all were over. Now it was kill or be killed where the alternatives were big money or no money. Something like that, on a significantly uglier and more lethal scale, occurred among Jack Egan's underworld clientele in the 1920s.

By the start of that decade Egan had built a reputation as the man to call if a gangster got in trouble, and that reputation extended far beyond the boundaries of Dayton. He was fearless, aggressive, savvy and persuasive. He was also in a geographic location that was perfect for his clientele. Between Dayton and Cincinnati was the city of Hamilton in Butler County. Hamilton became known as Little Chicago, and Butler County became infamous as a gathering place for bootleggers and other gangsters. What started as a local situation in which the law tended to look the other way accelerated over time as the area drew an increasingly ruthless and lethal breed of men. The accelerating level of violence in Little Chicago is partly reflected in the fact that between 1919 and 1927 nine law officers were murdered there. There is no accurate count of the deaths of private citizens. In the 1960s, a bailiff of the County Common Pleas Court told me that he had made good money in the 1920s converting guns to automatic firing weapons for those boys from Chicago.

It is one thing to be a stellar forensic performer where you pound on the facts if the facts favor your client, pound on the law if the law favors your client, and pound on the table if neither the facts nor the law are helpful. Gangsters who could find no solace in either facts or law and who were smart enough to know that pounding on the table would be a futile gesture needed more than legal skills. Their only hope was the trial that was prevented by missing witnesses or by pliable representatives of law enforcement or the judiciary.

Another complicating factor, especially to someone like Jack who never paid much attention to problems presented by conflicts of interest in the representation of multiple parties, was the increasing lack of brotherhood among thieves. Turf wars and personal grudges were increasingly common in the ranks of potential clients, and there was an alarming tendency to settle disputes with machine guns instead of diplomacy, mediation, arbitration or trial. Add to these concerns the risk that a client might become discontented with his lawyer's fee or his lawyer's performance.

Jack had a beautiful house on Route 48 north of Union, Ohio in Randolph Township. Like Macbeth's castle it was next to some woods. It featured a separate cottage where Jack met from time to time with some of the leading members of the underworld. And it featured a tunnel leading to the woods, a convenient escape route if a client or another visitor came calling at an unwelcome time.

Jack's wife, Nellie, remained in the house until she sold it in 1944. Until his own death in 1936, Jack remained in the eyes of all beholders a man impervious to danger. It seems probable, however, that, like Macbeth he became tormented by the path his ambition had taken. He had simply waded in blood so far that going back was no different from continuing forward. It is no wonder that Jack had an escape tunnel at his home in Union or that—despite his aggressive exterior—he had developed a tendency to glance over his shoulder while strolling on the sidewalk and to pick the seat with its back to the wall in public settings.

An example of the new breed of gangster is presented by the personality and exploits of a native of Cincinnati who ultimately made it in big time crime as a hitman with some twenty-one or more murders to his credit. While serving in the Army in World War I Raymond "Crane Neck" Nugent had become a buddy of Fred Burke and Bob Carey. That trio ended up in St. Louis in a gang which, with no known connection to Jack Egan, was known as "Egan's Rats." That gang had fallen apart in the mid-1920s when one of its members became a real rat who provided a prison habitat for a dozen of his peers following a mail robbery. Crane Neck then made a name for himself in the Dayton-Hamilton-Cincinnati territory as a bootlegger, armed robber and killer.

In 1925, Nugent outperformed the missing witness defense that Jack Egan had used to the advantage of Henry Hagelganz in 1912. A taxi driver named Red Weber had witnessed the murder of a bootlegger named Edward Schief at a cabaret in the Lee Hotel in Hamilton. A bootlegging associate of Schief was badly beaten in the incident, and Schief's wife ultimately committed suicide. Crane Neck, along with two other defendants, was indicted for murder. Using Egan's old habeas corpus trick Crane Neck was released on bond by a probate judge, but he was back in captivity in time for trial. The trial had to be continued because the key

Raymond "Crane Neck" Nugent.

witness, Mr. Weber, failed to appear. Found and jailed as a material witness, Weber went on the witness stand when the trial finally took place. Weber had provided the grand jury with a detailed and definitive statement which clearly showed Nugent to be the murderer he was alleged to be.

Never underestimate the power of intimidation. When Weber sat in the witness chair before the judge, the jury, the defendant, and the defendant's counsel, he suddenly didn't know anything about Nugent or the crime. He testified that his memory wasn't very good, that he had been sick for five or six years, and that he drank a great deal until recently. If he told the grand jury that Crane Neck murdered Schief, what he had said was not correct. The judge was compelled to direct the jury to return a not guilty verdict in favor of Crane Neck and his co-defendants. One of those co-defendants was named John Todd Messner. We will hear more about Crane Neck and Messner later. Weber's memory may have been bad, but at least it was not obliterated by a machine gun lobotomy.

While the missing witness ploy worked well for Crane Neck Nugent, Jack Egan was less successful in his attempt to borrow a ploy that retired Judge Ulysses Martin had used in stealing a verdict in a case prosecuted by Albert Scharrer. The case was known as the Chinese Tong Murder Case. Like many criminal cases, the outcome turned on eyewitness identification of the defendant.

In those somewhat racist days neither the eyewitness nor the jurors were of Chinese extraction. When the eyewitness was on the witness stand and asked to identify the murderer, the wily old defense lawyer had filled the courtroom with male Chinese spectators. It was impossible for the eyewitness to pick the right face out of the crowd, and the defendant was found not guilty. A similar ploy had worked for Jack, as you may remember, in the arrest of three out of a multitude of black party goers at the Bungaloo Club in his early days at Cockroach Castle.

When Jack some years later found himself defending a murder case where the evidence turned on the defendant's identification by an eyewitness, he found a man in Cleveland who looked almost exactly like his client. He arranged to have the double come to Dayton with the strategy of having him sit next to the defendant during the trial. For once the Dayton Police got a step ahead of Jack. They arrested the double on a trumped-up charge when he arrived at the Dayton train station. By the time the double was released from jail, he no longer looked anything like the defendant. Jack had to come up with another gimmick.

While murder may be every reader's favorite subject in the lexicon of criminal justice, it is not the only pathway to death or the only pastime of defense counsel. Unusual in its day and non-existent since the Supreme Court's decision in *Roe v. Wade* which legalized its subject matter, illegal abortions were often performed in appalling conditions which led to prosecutions. In the early 1960s, some Dayton gangsters had a business which brought women from as far away as St. Louis and Kansas City to obtain illegal abortions in Dayton. When the septic results of such procedures began filling the women's section of Miami Valley Hospital, a prosecution of the offending doctor was attempted. It collapsed in a deal that put the gang out of the illegal abortion business. In 1928, Jack Egan was called upon to defend a local African-American doctor when a nineteen-year-old lady from Troy died following an illegal operation. Society learned the hard way that prohibiting the consumption of alcohol does not stop people from drinking. It should remain hopeful that efforts to consign abortions back to the realm of illegality does not simply resurrect the grim days of illegal abortions.

The Volstead Act was, of course, the federal government's great contribution to the creation of organized crime in America and to the workload of criminal defense attorneys. If George Remus of Cincinnati gained a reputation as the king of Ohio bootleggers, Jack Egan wore a similar crown among the ranks of those who labored to keep the practitioners of that art out of court and out of jail. Many judges who, despite their personal consumption of liquid contentment, pronounced prison sentences on the bootleggers who appeared in their courts must have felt the pangs of hypocrisy. It was not a good era for cultivating a public respect for the law.

In the fall of 1922, fourteen men were indicted in Dayton as involved in a bootlegging ring conspiracy to violate the Volstead Act. Eleven of them went to trial in January 1923. Ten went to the jury after one was dismissed at the conclusion of testimony on a finding of insufficient evidence. Seven of the ten were found guilty. The defendants were big businessmen, not a handful of country folk with backyard stills. The ring had acquired 190,000 gallons of alcohol from the federal government to be denatured for legal uses. Instead, the alcohol was shipped to various cities to be sold to bootleggers and used to manufacture illegal whiskey. One shipment to Dayton consisted of one hundred barrels of alcohol. It provided a field day for Dayton attorneys, although two of those attorneys found themselves in disbarment proceedings, one for suborning perjury and one for converting to his own use money that had been posted for bonds.

Jack Egan avoided such pitfalls, and he burnished the reputation he had developed with his early century writs of habeas corpus as the man who achieves success in the art of releasing criminals. In 1925, he used that writ to secure an extradition hearing for a gentleman named Walter Nolan who was arrested on behalf of authorities from Hartford, Connecticut for violating his parole from the Connecticut State Penitentiary. Nolan, who had a history of twenty-two arrests for various crimes, had come from Connecticut to Ohio only to be convicted for violating the Volstead Act. Like many others of his breed, he would have nodded his head in assent to Ma Rainey's blues commentary that "thirty days ain't long when you're free to spend them as you choose, but it seems like a lifetime in the jailhouse where there ain't no booze." Keeping the likes of Mr. Nolan out of the jailhouse was no easy task.

While bootlegging may have been front and center on the criminal dockets of courts in the 1920s, there were still plenty of old-time burglars and safe crackers to vary the menu. A notorious bandit named Cowboy Hill posed a particular problem of potential prejudice when he was tried on a charge of having burglar tools in his possession. As Jack would later learn in the Rabbit Man Wilson case, it is difficult enough to explain why your client owns a case of nitroglycerin, an array of fuses, metal hammers, metal crowbars, and the like. It is even more difficult to explain why your client has to be on a stretcher in the courtroom as a result of the gun battle with police which attended his capture and arrest in September 1920. The Cowboy—whose real last name was Muzzio—doesn't exactly stir up images of Roy Rogers or Gene Autry. He first encountered Egan after his gang had robbed the West Carrollton bank back in April 1920 in the company of another bandit named Red McGahan.

The bad news upon Cowboy Hill's arrival at the Ohio State Penitentiary in February 1921, aside from the fact that the doctors said he would never be able to walk again, was the announcement by Warden Thomas that before he started to serve his one-to-twenty-five-year sentence he would have to serve out the unexpired sentences for two other crimes from which he had been placed on parole. That would stretch his stay until 1951 if he could live that long. I don't think that he did. The good news is that he would be in the same habitat as his old partner Dick Howell who was on murderers' row awaiting review by the Ohio Supreme Court of his conviction for slaying a Canton, Ohio plainclothes detective.

Another colorful client represented by Jack Egan in the 1920s was Red McGahan who would later join Hill and Howell as an inhabitant of the Ohio State Penitentiary. McGahan, but for the publicity accorded John Dillinger by the self-promoting J. Edgar Hoover, might top the all-time list of famous American bank robbers. Like Dillinger, banks in Ohio and Indiana were his specialty and he always got away. Like Dillinger, his career was brought to a close by the unfortunate fact that love is blind. Like Dillinger, he was considered an exceedingly dangerous gangster, an opinion confirmed by the presence of twenty law enforcement officers guarding him on a train ride to Dayton from Toledo where he had entered a plea on a charge of conspiracy to defraud the federal government on March 12, 1924. McGahan had amassed a long list of bank robberies, an estimated $500,000 in proceeds from those adventures, and two dead police officers who were murdered after a 1922 bank robbery in Grand Rapids. On one occasion, in a typical display of bravado, he had robbed a bank in Erie, Pennsylvania just two hours after being released on bond in that city on a charge of carrying a concealed weapon.

Red McGahan had sworn that he would never be taken alive. Never say never. He fell in love with a pretty girl from Parkersburg, West Virginia. In late 1923, he met her for lunch at a restaurant in Marietta, Ohio where orders were taken and filled as customers passed along the food counter. As he carried his food tray with both hands from the food counter to the cashier, he was suddenly jumped upon by a team of private detectives. He dropped the tray, but he didn't have time to pull his 32-special from his pocket and shoot his way out of the restaurant. At the time of his capture, he was a wanted man in a number of jurisdictions including Dayton, Ohio where he had robbed the West Carrollton bank in April 1920.

McGahan's trial for that 1920 robbery began in Judge Patterson's big court room on April 4, 1924. The prosecutor was Albert Scharrer who had cut his teeth in Jack Egan's office. McGahan was represented by Jack Egan who brought his old crony Jake Nevin in as his co-counsel. Nevin had been the county prosecutor from 1905 to

1908, and he would in 1929 become the first federal district judge to sit in Dayton. McGahan and his counsel thought they would avoid the one-to-fifteen year prison sentence for bank robbery by the two-year sentence in a more comfortable federal penitentiary that should result from the plea and conviction in Toledo. We will encounter some clever lawyering by Scharrer in the Rabbit Man Wilson case later in the decade. His ploy in the Red McGahan case was to persuade the federal judge in Toledo to impose a two-hour sentence instead of a two-year sen-

Albert Scharrer.

tence and bring the prisoner in custody to Dayton and the trial for bank robbery.

Egan and Nevin pulled out the old standby of a writ of habeas corpus and argued that the federal jurisdiction over the defendant trumped the right of the state court to put him to trial. The two-hour ploy killed that gambit both at trial and on appeal. Another legal issue arose early in the trial when it was discovered that one of the jurors had been a member of the grand jury which had indicted McGahan. That issue likewise brought no relief for the bank robber who, like an Elizabethan bear, was tied to the stake with no hope of eluding his attackers. Despite the three-year gap between the West Carrollton bank robbery and the Dayton trial, there were insurmountable obstacles to avoiding a conviction. McGahan had not simply robbed the bank. After accomplishing that task he had locked the bank's cashier and assistant cashier in the bank vault, assuring that they would never forget him. Abundant evidence of prior similar bank robberies put additional nails in the coffin of the defense case. Love may have caused King Edward to leave the throne. It didn't do much for Red McGahan or for John Dillinger either.

Like Cowboy Hill, McGahan received a warm greeting from Warden Thomas when he arrived at the Ohio State Penitentiary. He had spent eight years there ending in his release on parole in 1915. He thus had enjoyed only a little more than another eight years to pursue his impressive criminal career. Warden Thomas pointed out that McGahan would be one of the best of the many prisoners classified in the vernacular as "Bad Babies." "He's well-disciplined and knows to obey orders," said the Warden. Old soldiers just fade away.

SCENE 4:
The Rabbit Man

Jack Egan was the defense lawyer in the last case that Albert Scharrer tried as county prosecutor. The defendant was Jimmy "Rabbit Man" Wilson, a nationally known burglar who was arrested when he claimed a briefcase hidden under the steps at a vacant house. The briefcase was full of blasting caps and other items which were hardly the contents for which such luggage is designed, but perhaps not surprising material for a typical Egan client to take to work! When the jury had the audacity to bring in a "guilty" verdict, Jack's reaction was like that of Macbeth on seeing Banquo's ghost at an anticipated feast. Jack had become king, and his office may have been the modern version of Dunsinane. But he had a vision of a future when one of his associates would take his place.

The case is memorable, not only because of the colorful character of the defendant, but also as an example of the ingenuity of Jack Egan and the matching ingenuity of his adversary. Jack's client was indicted under a statute which made it a crime for any person to "have in his possession or control any cartridge, shell, bomb or other similar device, charged or filled with one or more explosives, intending to use the same or cause the same to be used for an unlawful purpose…" Jack was successful in avoiding a conviction of Counts 1 and 3 of a three count indictment under that statute, but his client was found guilty of the second count which charged him with possession and control of twenty-three detonating nitro explosive blasting caps with the intent to use them for an unlawful purpose. Jack's argument was that these were not explosives within the meaning of the statute and that, in any event, no license is required under the Ohio statutes for possession of blasting caps in quantities of less than one thousand. There was also no direct evidence of what purpose Jack's client had for the blasting caps. Jack was also able to present positive character testimony on behalf of his client from a number of Toledo policemen who came to Dayton to testify for him. What more could you ask than a blessing from law enforcement for your client's good character?

There was, however, the psychological problem of explaining circumstances that did not exactly display Jack's client as a model citizen. And there was also a physical problem. The stress of his practice had impacted Jack's health and stamina, and his physician had told him not to participate in courtroom trials for at least three months. He nonetheless rose to his task with what the newspaper described as "Celtic tenacity and fearlessness," and he gave one of the most dramatic closing arguments of his career. As that argument reached its climax, Judge Alfred McCray interrupted him to indicate that his allotted forty-five minutes were about over. "The Judge tells me my time is about up," Jack told the jury. He went on to say, "You can take that two ways. My time on the earth is about up." If the jury had no sympathy for his client, perhaps it would have some sympathy for his client's lawyer.

When the jury found against the defendant Jack took an appeal. In an appellate decision written by Judge James I. Allread and joined by Judges H. L. Ferneding and Albert H. Kunkle, the judgment entered on the jury's verdict was affirmed. The facts of the case were simple. In December of 1926, a citizen as agent for his mother visited a vacant residence owned by his mother on South Ludlow Street in Dayton. He noticed that the rear steps leading to the porch had been displaced. He found hidden under the steps a briefcase or bag. He called the police who took the bag to police headquarters where the following contents were discovered: a sledge hammer, brace, drills, pliers, twenty-three blasting caps wrapped in cloth, five blasting caps with wire attached, wrapped in cloth, two loaded revolvers, a coil or fuse and a bottle filled with a yellowish liquid in a wood container which was also wrapped in cloth. The police put the bag back under the porch and waited and watched until the defendant arrived and picked up the bag. At that point the police picked up the defendant. Shortly thereafter the defendant picked Jack to defend him.

The appellate court distinguished the licensing portion of the statute from the criminal section which referred only to "one or more" with respect to the number of explosives. It considered the question whether the blasting caps were "explosives" within the meaning of the statute as a fact issue and noted that the trial transcript contained conflicting expert testimony on that subject. It was kind enough not to mention the common knowledge that countless Chinese railroad workers had been killed in explosions occurring when they hammered blasting caps into the Rocky Mountains, thereby giving rise to the common expression "a Chinaman's chance." On the issue of intent the Court of Appeals found that a nefarious purpose was "a reasonable inference from all the circumstances." Respectable businessmen are unlikely to hide their tools under the porch steps of a vacant house.

So much for Jack's failed ingenuity.

Let us turn to Albert Scharrer's ingenuity on behalf of the State. The three-count indictment and all the papers filed in the case did not name the defendant as Jim Wilson. The defendant was repeatedly identified as Jim Wilson, alias Marvin Tiffin Parks, alias James Andrew Wilson, alias James Cordano, alias James Wilson, alias J. O'Bryan. Such references could rationally be considered somewhat prejudicial to the defendant. To give Albert his due, he left out from the caption Wilson's nickname of "Rabbit Man" with its connotation of "sneaking, running and hiding," but the local press readily supplied that omission for an eager reading public.

Even more ingenious was the pursuit of the defendant with two additional indictments. The one that went to trial was for possession of explosives. If the State lost that case, however, it could have taken the defendant to a second trial without double jeopardy risk on a separate indictment for possession of burglary tools (the sledge hammer, brace, drills and pliers). And if the second shot failed, there was a third indictment for carrying concealed weapons (the two loaded revolvers in the bag). There was no requirement of consolidation of such indictments at the time, and Jack even had to file a motion for a ruling on which indictment would be the first to go to trial.

Albert had poisoned the well with six alias names for the defendant and he had laid a perfect trap line with two pop-up indictments if the first one failed. His term as county prosecutor ended shortly after the bag was discovered under the porch. He must have considered its contents a Christmas gift he could not refuse since he got himself appointed special prosecutor to take the defendant to trial in early 1927 when he was no longer the county prosecutor. Since the defendant was sentenced to one to twenty years at hard labor with a minimum sentence of ten years, it was not necessary to pursue the other indictments. Months after the affirmance from the Court of Appeals, those indictments were quietly dismissed by Nick Nolan who had succeeded Albert as county prosecutor.

Disappointed by the announcement of the adverse verdict in the Rabbit Man Wilson case Jack stated in court that he would not likely appear in a criminal case again. In a lifetime of dealing with broken promises, this was another promise that was not kept. He did, however, enlist Scharrer as his co-counsel in the last notable criminal case he tried—the postal telegraph murder case of 1935 which we will visit in due course.

SCENE 5:
The Pelican's Blood

Ogden Nash made fun of the pelican as a bird whose beak can hold more than its belly can. In the myths and heraldry popular in the Middle Ages, however, the pelican had an exalted status as a creature that willingly gave its own blood to nourish its offspring. It prefigured Christ himself whose body and blood was consumed by his flock on a regular basis at Holy Communion. You may have seen the famous pelican portrait of Queen Elizabeth I who reigned in England's Golden Age.

With this background there is a significant element of irony in the fact that the seminal event in the next episode of Jack Egan's career took place in a pool hall in North College Hill known as the Pelican Club. A lot of blood flowed as a result of that event, but the donors who provided it were not making voluntary sacrifices for the good of their fellow citizens. The date is April 8, 1928. The key players are five masked bandits who in the course of a robbery at the club murdered a well-liked Village Marshall named Peter Dumele and wounded another patron of the establishment. The five key players discharged the contents of two sawed-off shotguns and several revolvers. One shotgun blast took off poor Mr. Dumele's right hand and shattered his arm. Another hit him square in the chest. According to the best sources available, the five key players were Rodney Ford, John Todd Messner, Breck Lutes, Jack Parker and Robert Zwick (known as the Fox).

By early October, Ford, Messner, and Lutes had all been arrested. Ford was sitting in his car in Hamilton when officers apprehended him. He dropped a revolver into the backseat of the car and surrendered. Whether by chance or otherwise, Messner was arrested at a fishing camp near Excello, Jack Egan's boyhood home. He was in the company of Dago Rose Myers, a lady we will later encounter as the sweetheart of Bob Zwick. Seventeen Hamilton and Middletown police along with Butler County Sheriff's Department deputies participated in his arrest, and for some reason he presented a black eye at his arraignment. Parker and Zwick eluded capture, although Parker's dead and bullet-ridden body was in early May found near Lebanon, Ohio. It was rumored that his unhappy ending was caused by Zwick with the help of his then buddy Ray "Crane Neck" Nugent out of concern that Mr. Parker might provide some unfortunate testimony if apprehended by police. Remember Crane Neck and the silenced witness from that 1925 murder case?

Ford was the first to go to trial on a charge of first-degree murder. Sometime before the trial he had contacted Jack Egan to represent him, but Egan was tied up in another case. Even Jack Egan lacked the ability to be in two places at once. Ford's trial commenced in mid-December 1928. On the night of the first day of trial the State's star witness, a young man named Robert Andres who had the misfortune of being at the right place at the wrong time on the night of the murder, was silenced by death. That event prompted the resignation of Ford's trial attorney and an emergency call to Jack Egan who was engaged in an unrelated trial in Dayton. Jack came to Hamilton after his Dayton court session and conferred with the judge and the prosecutor. He indicated that he was willing to take over Ford's defense if the trial could be continued until mid-January 1929.

The judge declined to continue the trial or to declare a mistrial based on the death of the State's star witness. He appointed two Cincinnati attorneys to handle the defense of Ford, and Jack—who lacked any other available manpower—sent Carl Heindel, a Dayton lawyer who served as the librarian of the Dayton Law Library, to monitor the trial. The dead witness had testified and been subjected to cross-examination at a preliminary hearing. The judge accordingly permitted his testimony to be read to the jury. The reading was reported as having the solemn effect of hearing a voice from the grave.

Ford testified that he did not know any of the other alleged participants in the crime, that he was at home coloring Easter eggs with his wife and children the night before the shooting, and that he was still at home with his family when the shooting occurred. He tried to put Messner and Lutes on the witness stand to testify that they did not know him, but this attempt was blocked by their attorneys who respectfully declined to permit them to testify. In fact, at the time of Ford's trial, Messner was being tried in an adjoining courtroom for shooting two Cincinnati policemen in a totally unrelated incident.

Ford was convicted of first-degree murder and sentenced to death. Separate subsequent trials of Messner and of Lutes resulted in convictions and the imposition of a life sentence for each of them. Jack Parker remained dead, and Bob Zwick maintained his status as a fugitive from justice. When the dust cleared, Jack Egan reentered the story to handle Ford's appeal with the assistance of Jack's legal associate Charlie Brennan. In 1936, Charlie would be interviewed by the FBI. He provided interesting information about Jack's relationship with members of the Dayton police force and a certain Common Pleas judge as well as his representation of such notable gangsters as Bob Zwick and Jew Bates of whom you shall hear more in due time. Jack's appellate efforts on behalf of Rodney Ford were based on the trial court's failure to grant a continuance or a mistrial when the prejudicial event of the death of the State's key witness and the withdrawal of the defendant's trial attorney occurred on the first day of trial. It was also based on a claim of simple fairness: if two of the responsible parties received life sentences, it just wasn't fair to put the third responsible party in the electric chair.

When the appellate courts did not purchase what Jack was selling, Jack went to the governor's office with the same zeal and tenacity we have seen him display in earlier cases. His reference in his presentation to the governor to the death of poor Mr. Andres, the State's star witness, as a "disappearance" could fairly be construed as gilding the lilies at Mr. Andres' funeral. The facts are that, on the night before he was scheduled to testify in the Ford murder trial, Andres was stabbed and shot multiple times. His body was then rushed from northern Kentucky to the site of an abandoned barbecue shack in Ohio where it was bathed in kerosene. Then both the body and the barbecue shack were totally consumed by flames. In potential defense of Jack's argument, this certainly does qualify as a disappearance.

The Pelican's blood continued to flow after the murders of Marshall Dumele, the bootlegger Jack Parker, and poor Mr. Andres. On December 18, 1920, a thousand "wanted" posters were printed and disseminated with descriptions and pictures of Zwick and Nugent as suspects in the Andres slaying. A $2,500 reward was offered. Another Hamilton gangster, Robert Kolker, who was a friend of Jack Parker, was shot and seriously wounded by the overly aggressive team of Nugent and Zwick. It was another machine gun volley into Kolker's moving automobile. There was apparently concern that Kolker, like Parker, might implicate Nugent and Zwick in the murder of Andres.

On May 20, 1929, a gangster named George Murphy was stood up against a garage wall in Hamilton's Third Ward and perforated with eighteen machine gun bullets. Murphy's current sweetheart, an attractive young lady named Pauline Wilson, was on the same date killed in a rooming house in Hamilton. Her body was thrown into the Great Miami River. By the time it was found, she was no longer attractive. These murders were a product of a bootleg war between

Murphy and a long time Hamilton bootlegger and hijacker named Turkey Joe Jacobs. Jacobs engaged Zwick as his hitman, a move that broke up the team of Zwick and Nugent. In another bad moment on May 27, 1928, a week after the deaths of Murphy and Wilson, Zwick was driving down Symmes Corner Road, five miles from Hamilton, with his friend Turkey Joe Jacobs when Nugent in a passing car unloaded a fusillade of machine gun fire which put sixteen bullet holes in Turkey Joe's head and some other holes in Zwick. With Nugent in the assailants' car was Fats Wrassman who in turn was shot to death sometime later in Hamilton by a sheriff's investigator. There may have been another man in that car, but he remains unknown.

Somehow Zwick managed to escape from his car with blood streaming down his face and one finger dangling by its skin. He was later picked up by a young man to whom he fabricated the story that he had been in a car wreck with his girlfriend and didn't want to call the police because he didn't want his wife to know that he was running around with another woman. The Pelican's blood didn't stop flowing until April 1933, when Zwick was tried and convicted of the

murder of Andres back in 1928. In the interim he and Dago Rose had been on an odyssey that took them many places from the home base they had acquired in, of all places, Dayton, Ohio. Rose gave tearful testimony for him in vain at his murder trial. He also testified at the trial, but he had to talk out of the side of his mouth since his jaw was wired shut as a result of wounds he received in a shootout with police when he was arrested in Toledo. At the time of her testimony Rose was residing at the women's penitentiary in Marysville, Ohio, after a conviction

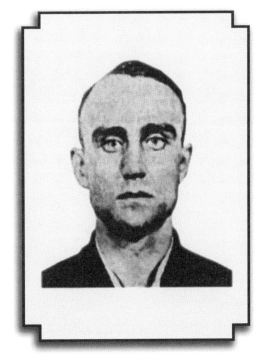

Bob Zwick

for harboring a felon. At least that was a residence preferable to the cell on death row that resulted from Zwick's long overdue court proceeding.

After the Turkey Joe murder, Nugent went to Chicago with his record of some twenty-one murders and became elevated to the status of a hitman for the Capone mob. According to the best available evidence he became one of the executioners who put Bugs Moran out of business by killing seven members of Moran's gang in the St. Valentine's Day Massacre on February 14, 1929. After that infamous moment Crane Neck followed Al Capone's brother, Ralph, to Miami, Florida, where he ran a tavern for a while and then disappeared. The word on the street was that he started buying booze from a Capone competitor and was fed to an alligator in the Everglades. Twenty years later the wife he left behind in Ohio went to the probate court in Cincinnati to have him declared dead so that she could collect the $1,500 pension owing from his service in World War I.

ACT V

Map of Union, Ohio, and Egan's home.

The Years of Life Noir

We now enter the last chapter of Jack Egan's strange, eventful life. We will encounter the sere, the yellow leaf. As with Macbeth, the leap of vaulting ambition to immersion in a dangerous world, the efforts to make ends justify means, had triggered an endless repetition of encounters with violence. It had become a petty pace of tomorrow and tomorrow and tomorrow. Before the church bell rang for the last service, however, there were some further representations of infamous clients and the brightening of a last memorable trial—the song of a swan at the edge of mortality.

SCENE 1:
The Beast and the Beauty

As the last decade of his career came into view Jack Egan acquired an impressive client who even as seasoned a criminal defense lawyer as Jack would be wise to feed with a long-handled spoon. Charlie Brennan, as honest a lawyer as ever breathed Dayton air, confirmed Jack's representation of a gangster known as Jew Bates. Bates had a long record as a hitman and had served as chief lieutenant for Dean O'Banion, a soft-spoken florist who was known in the Chicago underworld as a brilliant arranger both of bouquets and of homicides.

There were several clashes between O'Banion who ruled the north side of Chicago and Al Capone who ruled the south side. Jew Bates was the cause of one of those clashes. O'Banion had made him the manager of a speakeasy known as the Hawthorne Smoke Shop in which Capone had an ownership interest. Bates apparently was an excellent manager until he caught the gambling bug that was common to the patrons of that establishment. He began betting against the house himself, and he was reported to have won $55,000 in a one-month period. Capone was incensed and, with support of other investors, told O'Banion that "the Jew is through." O'Banion's reply was, "not on your life; he is going to stay." And stay he did, until a convoy of loaded limousines pulled up in front of O'Banion's flower shop in November 1924. Blown away by friends of Capone while he was pruning flowers in his shop, O'Banion was blessed in death by an opulent funeral that would be remembered for decades as the ultimate bootleggers' farewell.

O'Banion's death left Jew Bates temporarily out of a job. It is difficult to trace his steps from November 1924 to February 1929. At some point when he was using the name George Karl, Bates faked his own death to avoid a Wisconsin indictment. But what better vocation could there have been than to find a new job with the man who had taken O'Banion's place. Bugs Moran had taken over the bootleg business in Chicago's north side. By the way, Bugs' last clash with the criminal justice system resulted in a trial in Dayton, Ohio, in 1945, followed by a guilty verdict and a trip to the Ohio State Penitentiary. Jack Egan was dead by the time of that trial, but he did outlive Jew Bates who in the wake of the massacre on February 14, 1929, that eliminated seven members of Bugs Moran's mob traveled the well-worn path that leads from Chicago to Dayton and Hamilton, Ohio.

Al Capone always had an alibi when questioned about the St. Valentine's Day massacre, but it is generally understood that he was behind that elimination of another competitor in his growing business. Several theories have been offered as to the identity of the machine gunners who pulled the triggers at that infamous event. The most probable is that they were Al Capone's American boys, Crane Neck Nugent and his World War I buddies Fred Burke and Bob Carey along with Gus

Winkeler. As Bugs Moran himself said, "only Capone kills like that." The event was a good reason for Bates' timely relocation to Jack Egan's territory.

Fortunately or unfortunately, Bates did not provide his Ohio attorney much of an opportunity to demonstrate his forensic skill in a big jury trial. Within a month or so after the St. Valentine's Day massacre Bates and two other men were arrested at a Hamilton hotel. All three had guns, but a loitering charge was not much of a challenge to their counsel. Information provided to the police by members of the Bob Zwick gang in the spring of 1930, after Bates had found another and perhaps better world, indicated that Bates and a friend of his named Larry Coates had teamed up with Zwick and his crew who were involved in at least five murders and three bank robberies as 1929 ran its course. Bates and Coates, without the company of Zwick, then surfaced again in Ohio. They were arrested on December 14, 1929, on charges resulting from a robbery that had taken place in Newport, Kentucky, six weeks earlier. They were apparently asleep when the arrest occurred. A loaded revolver was found under Bates' pillow, but he surrendered without any incident. Despite records of previous arrests of both men, Egan's patented process of habeas corpus put them back on the streets of Cincinnati.

On December 19, Bates and Coates got into an argument in the lobby of the Cincinnati hotel at which they were attempting to register under false names. The other party to the altercation was a rival gangster named John Marcus. Marcus jumped on Bates as soon as he saw him and asserted that Cincinnati was not big enough to hold both of them. A revolver was displayed in the ensuing struggle. Bates and Coates had already been ordered out of the hotel for giving false names in attempting to register. The fighting trio lurched out of the hotel and disappeared into an adjacent alley.

While we don't know what happened in the alley, we do know that all three survived the altercation. And we also know that they didn't survive it for very long. Bates and Coates crossed the river and took up residence at the Vendor Home Hotel in Newport, Kentucky. On December 24, they failed to show up for their scheduled arraignment in the Cincinnati police court. In retrospect arraignment and incarceration would have been an excellent option for them. On January 6, 1930, their bullet-ridden bodies were found on the steps of Booth Memorial Hospital where they had been unceremoniously dumped out of a passing automobile. Coates survived his wounds. Bates died the day after he arrived at the hospital. There was another gangster named Stubbs who was taken to St. Elizabeth Hospital shortly after the bodies of Bates and Coates were dumped on the steps of Booth Hospital. The most likely story that has been pieced together from the various accounts of events given by Stubbs and Coates is that the gangland feud which surfaced in the lobby of the Cincinnati hotel was reasserted when Marcus and Stubbs got into a running gun battle in one car with Bates and Coates who were in another car.

This time Bates' death was not faked. His funeral was held in Chicago, but it wasn't as fancy as the one provided six years earlier in Chicago for his boss Dean O'Banion. Coates' girlfriend, however, was quoted as saying that she got a big bang out of seeing a newspaper account of the involvement of Bates in a $23 robbery since she had seen him on multiple occasions giving an orchestra leader $50 to play a requested number. Bates was, in fact, in his short career as notable and dangerous a hitman as Crane Neck Nugent. He was well known as a killer since his early days as Dean O'Banion's chief lieutenant. He was known in the underworld as a lone wolf who usually worked at his trade without accomplices, a physically powerful man, a dangerous opponent in a fight who had no scruples and fought with any means at hand. His name was the first to be linked by law enforcement definitely with the wholesale beer war killings that had closed down virtually every saloon in Chicago.

A beast without a beauty would not be nearly as fascinating, and there was indeed a beauty—as well as our Dayton lawyer—associated with this beast. The beauty in question had been a mourner at the O'Banion funeral and again at the Jew Bates funeral. She had been the sweetheart of each of those men at the times of their respective deaths. Her name was Margaret Collins, and her kiss was definitely the kiss of the spider woman. The funerals of O'Banion and Bates were only two of the eight funerals she attended as the sweetheart of the decedent. All eight of those lost lovers met their deaths either by police or gang guns. Her concupiscence career earned her the name of Mad Meg, the Queen of the Gang World. It is difficult to decide whether tears or envious sighs are the appropriate reactions to the story of her life.

The aftermath of the gangland demise of Jew Bates, while it has little to do with the career of Jack Egan, adds to an understanding of the increasingly brutish world in which Jack plied his profession. Coates was charged with shooting to kill Stubbs, but Stubbs was unable to provide a positive identification of him. The charge could not survive a trip to a grand jury, and Coates retained his freedom for whatever that was worth. On January 22, 1931, a prospective purchaser of a vacant

Margaret Collins.

house three miles north of Hamilton found the body of John Marcus, the probable slayer of Jew Bates. The body was bound with wire and partially decomposed. It was located in a secret cellar in the house that had previously contained a still. The body contained two bullets.

In February 1931, Coates was arrested in Florida for questioning by law enforcement from Covington, Kentucky regarding his activities in Covington. On his arrest his revolver was confiscated. Ballistic tests demonstrated that the bullets found in the rotting body of John Marcus had been fired from that gun. Coates never had to answer, at least to law enforcement, for that murder. In the early morning hours of July 20, 1931, he was driving his father back to Cincinnati from a Sunday afternoon at a fishing camp on the Little Miami River. As he reached the city limits of Cincinnati, another car pulled alongside his. A shotgun blast from that car ended the career and the life of Larry Coates.

Whether or not Bates, Marcus and Coates now rest in peace, I am hopeful that someday you and I will. There appears to be little positive that can be said about

Jew Bates. The fact that he was numbered among the clients of Jack Egan nevertheless added to Egan's reputation as the man to see if you were a gangster—or for that matter a mere unfortunate citizen in trouble with the law—in Ohio or northern Kentucky.

SCENE 2:
The Games Continue

The last six years of Jack Egan's life were not totally consumed in a frenzied atmosphere of flying bullets and flowing blood. The triumvirate of Dayton lawyers who met Egan at Eve and Dick Williams' saloon when he arrived in Dayton remained major players on Dayton's legal scene. Carroll Sprigg would outlive Jack by six years. Jake Nevin would preside as Dayton's federal district judge from 1929 until his death in 1952. The third member of that turn-of-the-century triumvirate had his two sons join him in the practice of law in the year that Nevin became a federal judge. You may remember one of those sons, Horace, in his high school educational role as Jack Egan's office boy. Roland Baggott had left the state court bench in 1926 and re-entered private practice. He remained Egan's friend and companion until the end, and he survived Egan's death by only two years. In 1933, they joined hands in a business venture that bore little relationship to the practice of law. It was called the Jockey Club, and it had a lively—if not long-lasting—history. It was the culmination of a well-established interest the two men had in the princely sport of horse-racing.

We know from the testimony at the 1920 Dayton gambling probe that Jack was magnetized to games of chance and to the betting excitement offered by the racetrack. He certainly had learned from his representation of Fred Gondorf that there are thin lines between greed and gullibility, between sophistication and stupidity, and between illusion and delusion. His less aristocratic clientele had certainly made it clear to him that where there are card games there will inevitably be marked cards, where there are dice games there will inevitably be loaded dice, and where there are horse races there will inevitably be fixes. If Gondorf's Big Con furnished a film script for *The Sting*, the story of the Jockey Club would have been a perfect subject for a W. C. Fields' film filled with dishonest men destined to be cheated and suckers who don't deserve an even break.

On August 2, 1933, incorporation papers were filed for Dayton Jockey Club Inc. by Roland W. Baggott and his son Horace W. Baggott. The papers indicate that the company issued 500 shares of stock with no par value. Jack Egan's obituary in 1936 noted that he was "one of the officials of the Dayton Jockey Club." The probate court inventory filed in his estate listed 250 shares in the Dayton Jockey Club appraised at no value. On August 30, 1933, the Ohio Racing Commission considered an application from the Dayton Jockey Club to provide horse races at the Montgomery County Fairgrounds from September 13 to October 14. That application was refused, but the commission did authorize the club to hold the horse races from September 30 to October 14. The dates were extended through October 21, and it was reported that "the races have been well attended and the betting has been comparatively heavy throughout the race meet."

After that auspicious beginning the club beat competitors from other local groups as well as groups from New Orleans, Chicago and Columbus to run twenty-nine days of horse races at the Dayton Fairgrounds in the summer of 1934. Judge Baggott was listed as president of the Club; Jack Egan was listed as the Vice-President and Treasurer; and Horace Baggott—"another of the Gem City's leading barristers"—was listed as secretary. An unhappy creditor from the 1933 season, however, threw the future of the enterprise into the realm of doubt with a lawsuit seeking the appointment of a receiver. Judge Baggott confirmed the Club's insolvency, but Judge Patterson solved the problem by appointing Jack Egan as receiver for the Club. The unhappy creditor carried his complaint to federal court with a petition in bankruptcy. After a hearing Judge Nevin dismissed the petition. He made no finding as to the amount of the indebtedness owing to the plaintiff, but he found that the assets of the Jockey Club were greatly in excess of the amount claimed. Shortly thereafter, Judge Patterson vacated the receivership with a finding that the Club is now solvent and is in no further need of a receiver.

The path was thus cleared for an exciting series of horse races in June 1934. The season was indeed exciting, at least in the jockey's room. On June 6 a request was made to Horace Baggott, now Treasurer as well as Secretary of the Club, for compensation for a jockey who was lying in a local hospital, penniless and nursing a broken leg sustained in a fall at one of the Club's races. The other jockeys threatened to go on strike if compensation was not provided. An altercation began between Horace and a horse trainer; the altercation escalated into a free-for-all in which some of the participants were thrown through a window. The paddock judge was rendered unable to continue his official duties, and he as well as several others required stitches and additional medical attention. The excitement continued when some jockeys were suspended, and an investigation of alleged fixing of races was initiated at the end of June. In what was probably an essay in understatement, it was reported that some of the races "have had a very suspicious appearance to horsemen and to the intelligent patrons of the course."

The Jockey Club failed to obtain the County Fairgrounds for horse races in 1935, but the Baggotts and Egan were undeterred in their quest to provide spectator sport and betting opportunities to the citizens of the community. It was reported in the fall of 1934 that they were in negotiations with General Motors to acquire by lease or purchase the old McCook airplane field as a race track site. The 1935 season proved just as exciting as the 1934 season, again for reasons of dubious merit. Its nineteen-day racing meet in June was interrupted for a day when the odds-on favorite and another heavily played horse failed to get away from the starting gate with the rest of the pack in a major race. A major race was thereby transmogrified into a major riot at the racetrack. The president of the Ohio Racing Commission conducted an investigation and recommended revocation of the Club's racing license. Valiant to the end, the Baggotts and Egan, when the Montgomery County Fair Board decided not to sanction the Jockey Club's proposed races in 1936, announced that they were considering acquiring the Dayton Speedway Track off of Germantown Pike as a new race site. Jack's race through life ended in 1936, however, and it is not surprising that his stock in the Jockey Club was inventoried as a valueless asset.

Egan's foray into the business of horse-racing was only a side show. The main tent in the 1930s still featured a three ring circus of amazing and amusing legal disputes. The side rings were the acrobats and trapeze artists engaged in civil suits and business ventures. In the last year of his life Jack incorporated the Russell's Point Resort Company which still dispenses libations and provides entertainment to partygoers on the shores of Lake Erie. Within a month of his death he filed a lawsuit against a negligent motorist to recover damages for the wrongful death of a thirteen-year-old girl. Since the only measure of damages for wrongful death in those days was financial loss to the next-of-kin, it seems unlikely that the case would have fueled Jack's retirement if he had lived long enough to take it to trial.

While most of the side-ring activities in Egan's legal circus were matters of significance only to those personally involved in them, one civil case bears mention since it involves a type of lawsuit that, thanks to the Ohio legislature, no longer exists. Even in the early 1960s it was not uncommon for the unpleasantness that universally attends divorce proceedings to be escalated by the filing of two types of civil suits. The first was a suit for alienation of affections against the third-party who had become romantically involved with a spouse. The other was a civil suit for "criminal conversation" against the spouse who became involved with that third party. When the defendants in such civil lawsuits were people of prominence in the community, the sordid details of allegations and evidence became—as might be expected—grist for the media mills.

The joint activities of Egan and the Baggotts were not confined to horse races. In 1932, they filed as co-counsel an alienation of affections lawsuit against a civic leader well known in Piqua and Miami County. Their claim charged that the defendant seduced their client's wife and rendered her so enamored with the defendant that she transferred her affections to him. The defendant reacted in typical style with charges of blackmail and defamation. He announced that he had hundreds of friends who held him in high regard and would vouch for him. The screams of outrage resulting from both sides of such disputes no longer are heard as subjects of independent litigation, but they are still popular pastimes in divorce proceedings despite the fact that they have become essentially irrelevant to the issues in those cases as well. When wedded bliss goes amiss, it is often impossible to avoid acrimony and recrimination even if such emotions have no legal consequence.

Whether fascinating or boring, the activities in the side rings of Jack's legal circus were never the main focus of his practice or of the public perception of that practice. The center ring was always the arena of mayhem and murder. In 1930, Jack extricated a gentleman named Eunash Doxey from a bank robbery charge when three key witnesses were unable to identify Doxey as one of the three men who committed the robbery. It proved a pyrrhic victory, however, since Doxey was immediately extradited to Campbell County, Kentucky on a charge of robbing a roadhouse. A good client, like a bad penny, just keeps coming back. And he usually has friends who are also potential clients. In the same year Jack found himself representing Tag Lee, another member of the Bob Zwick gang, on a charge of assault with intent to rob a bank.

In 1931, Jack represented a defendant charged with manslaughter as a result of an automobile accident. More in keeping with his usual clientele in criminal court was Harvey Landon, a client charged with impersonating a federal officer. He was alleged to be the "brains" of a gang of racketeers who were making life miserable for bootleggers in Dayton and southern Ohio by posing as prohibition officers and offering protection at a price against prosecution for violations of the Volstead Act. Landon was the operator of the Grand Hotel in Hamilton, and he had been the previous operator of the infamous Stockton Club south of Hamilton and the Garden of Allah on Dixie Highway. He thus had intimate knowledge of the activities of bootleggers and the ability to share such knowledge with genuine federal officers if protection money was not paid. One problem with gangsters is that they just don't seem able to trust one another!

Bootleggers, bank robbers, hitmen, petty and not so petty felons and miscreants—they all continued to find their way to the door of Jack's law office. In terms of Jack's continuing reputation, however, they were all merely forerunners to a man who would need and obtain his services in 1933.

SCENE 3:
America's First Public Enemy No. 1

Jack Egan was thirty years older than John Dillinger, the legendary bank robber destined to become the first person to be designated by J. Edgar Hoover as America's Public Enemy Number One. When Dillinger was released on May 10, 1933, after serving nine and a half years in the Indiana Reformatory and Indiana State Prison, he found himself drawn to the Dayton area. The first bank robbery of his career took place on June 21, 1933, in New Carlisle, a stone's throw from Dayton, and he developed a romantic relationship with Mary Longnaker who lived in a rooming house on First Street in downtown Dayton. On August 14, 1933, he robbed another Ohio bank in Bluffton, near Lima. In the same period he began his depredations among banks in small towns in Indiana.

At 1:30 a.m. on September 23, 1933, shortly after one of those Indiana bank robberies, he was roused from Mary's bedroom by the Dayton Police, arrested, and placed in the Third Street jail. When the police slowly opened the bedroom door, there was John Dillinger in the middle of the room looking at snapshots he had taken on a trip with Mary to the Chicago World's Fair. A tip from Mary's landlady about Mary's boyfriend thus brought a temporary end to Dillinger's four months of freedom and what appears to have been a permanent end to Mary's romance. Jack to the rescue. On September 26, 1933, a package arrived

John Dillinger and Mary Longnaker.

John Dillinger, Dayton mug shot.

at the Indiana State Prison containing the wherewithal for the escape of Charles Makley, Harry Pierpont, Russell Clark, and seven other men. The ones named were three of Dillinger's old prison buddies who had gone to crime school with him during his years of confinement. By October 3—one week later—they had robbed the bank in St. Mary's, Ohio and added $11,000 to their annual income.

On September 28, 1933, two days after the jailbreak occurred at the Indiana State Prison, Jack Egan had a chambers conference with Judge Patterson of the common pleas court in Dayton. They were joined by three officers who arrived from Lima with a warrant for Dillinger's arrest in connection with the Bluffton bank robbery. On the same afternoon Dayton attorney Hugh Altick received a call from a bank in Indiana which had been the subject of a robbery by Dillinger on the day of his Dayton arrest. The bank had learned of the arrest and undoubtedly wanted the fruits of the robbery that were probably in Dillinger's possession when he was arrested. "Don't worry," said Hugh, "I am well versed in the applicable law and will be in court on your behalf tomorrow with a writ of replevin in my hand." Hugh arrived in court as promised, only to find an entry signed by Judge Patterson in the clerk's office transferring Dillinger to Lima on the Bluffton arrest warrant and releasing all of the money in Dillinger's possession to Jack Egan.

A Dayton news reporter asked the clerk what happened to the money Dillinger had with him when he was booked. He was told he needed to talk to Jack Egan if he wanted an answer to that question. Here is the account published by that reporter in the *Dayton Daily News* on July 29, 1984, over fifty years after the events:

I returned to the press room and phoned Egan's office. He had just walked in. I asked him what had happened to the money.

'I got it,' he said in his high, squeaky voice.

'You got it?' I exclaimed, amazed. 'I don't understand. Wasn't that money supposed to be held for Indiana authorities, as evidence in the Indianapolis bank robbery?'

'I was paid that money for my fee,' he snapped, obviously irritated that I should ask such a question.

'Fee for what?' I persisted.

'Legal service,' he shouted, his voice higher. 'I got him transferred to Allen County where I will represent him on a false charge of bank robbery. I will also oppose any extradition proceedings if they are brought by Indiana.'

'But, that money was evidence,' I persisted.

'No one can prove that,' he snapped angrily. 'We will insist it was his life savings.'

'But some of those packages of currency were strapped with the Indianapolis bank wrappers,' I persisted.

'Never saw anything like that,' Egan retorted and hung up on me.

Fact or myth? Somehow, it has the ring of truth.

The story raises a host of other questions that are not as easy to answer. Did Dillinger believe that some of the "fee money" was designated as bribes to a judge or to a sheriff in Lima? Was any of it used for such purposes? Why was the sheriff in Lima surprised when three members of the Dillinger gang walked into his office and casually asked for Dillinger's release? Did Jack live the rest of his life in fear of retaliation for converting designated bribes over to his own use and benefit? All the people who might be able to answer any of these questions are dead, and I wasn't even born in 1933.

What we do know is that on October 12, 1933, the sheriff in Lima was shot to death, and Dillinger exited the Allen County Jail in the company of members of his gang. A word about the two members of the Dillinger gang who paid with their lives for that murder is in order. Harry Pierpont was the Douglas Fairbanks, Errol Flynn member of the gang, handsome, reckless and possessed with the killer

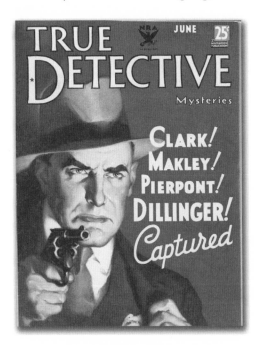
True Detective cover.

instinct. Charley Makley had an interesting Dayton connection. Roger Makley—a skilled, esteemed and very funny Dayton lawyer who had been the United States Attorney in Dayton and then a partner in a prestigious Dayton law firm—always claimed that Charley was the only member of his family who ever made a name for himself. I once gave Roger a copy of an edition of *True Detective Magazine* which had a lurid cover picture and an exciting article about Charley. I also checked the family tree back to the common ancestor of both and found that their ancestor died in 1859 leaving a comforting distance between Roger and his cousin Charley.

Back to the story. Jack remained, as far as I can tell, on the sidelines as the story of the Dillinger gang unfolded through 1933 and 1934. That story is well-documented. In March of 1933, poor Mary Longnaker was replaced as Dillinger's girlfriend by Billie Frechette who in turn later deferred to Polly Hamilton who was a friend of Anna Sage, the lady in red who precipitated the FBI assassination of Dillinger in Chicago on July 22, 1934. After the jail break in October of 1933, the gang went back to work in the bank robbery business. All were arrested on January 26, 1934, in Tucson, Arizona. Dillinger was sent to a small jail in Crown Point, Indiana from which he escaped on March 3, 1934 with a homemade false gun. Pierpont, Makley, and Clark were sent back to the prison from which they had escaped in Michigan City, Indiana. They were later extradited to Ohio where they awaited trial for the murder of the Lima sheriff.

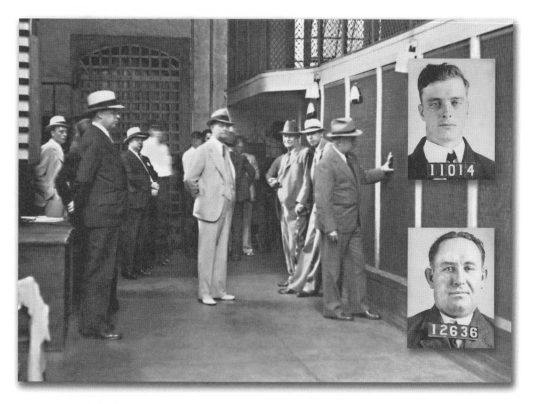

Harry Pierpont and Charles Makley. Death Row at the Ohio State Penitentiary.

The trials of Pierpont and Makley resulted in death penalty sentences and confinement in a most unpleasant part of that most unpleasant structure known as the Ohio State Penitentiary. Having little to lose and little to do on death row but await the inevitable, they decided to go out in a blaze of glory. They carved some pretty realistic-looking guns out of soapstone and used them to make a dramatic bid for freedom.

That bid resulted in a hail of gunfire on death row that was impossible to answer with guns made of soapstone. Makley was killed on the spot on September 22, 1934. Pierpont was badly shot up and begging for the coup de grâce. He was told "No, Harry, we're going to save your life so that we can put you into the electric chair," a promise they kept in the following month. In what may have been the only kind act of his life, Pierpont broke his silence before his execution to confirm that the sheriff in Lima was not bribed and did not willingly participate in Dillinger's escape.

Whether or not all these activities gave moments of tension to Jack Egan, he received a glorious Christmas present at the end of 1934. It set the stage for the glorious swan song at the end of his career—the trial of Louis Parker in March and April of 1935.

SCENE 4:
The Postal Telegraph Murder

Louis E. Parker was a policeman from Savannah, Georgia whose wife left him and ran off with her paramour to Dayton. On December 22, 1934, Parker resigned from the Savannah Police Department and left town. At 3:00 a.m. on December 24, 1934, he registered at a downtown Dayton hotel. Before leaving Georgia he had sent a ten dollar money order for his wife to the postal telegraph company in Dayton and asked that delivery of the order be withheld until 9:00 a.m. on the twenty-forth. On the morning of December 24, he went to the postal telegraph office, which was next to the county jail on West Third Street and asked if that was where money orders were cashed. Receiving an affirmative reply, he went across the street to a shoeshine parlor at the entrance of the Dayton Arcade, had his shoes shined, and waited. Later in the morning the lover of Parker's wife and her mother arrived at the postal telegraph company to claim and cash the money order. Parker crossed Third Street. He entered the telegraph office. Shots rang out. The lover of Parker's wife lay dead on the telegraph office floor in a pool of blood. The following day was not a happy Christmas day for

Louis Parker on the day of the shooting.

any of those involved in the family tragedy, although the wife's lover by then was oblivious to both joy and sorrow.

Jack was engaged to represent the defendant. He must have been thinking back to his successful defense of Hamilton Curry, the railroad detective, in Curry's 1909 murder trial. He must also have been thinking back to the performance of Albert Scharrer as his opposing attorney in his unsuccessful defense of the Rabbit Man Wilson trial. He enlisted Albert as his co-counsel. You can almost hear them as they analyzed the facts in their initial strategy session.

A man sets up a scheme to bring his wife to a certain place at a specific time. He gets a gun and travels a thousand miles to make sure that he is present at that time and place. The wife's lover arrives. The gun goes off. At first glance it sounds to the uninitiated like a fair case of premeditated murder—an offense that in the mid-1930s conjured immediate thoughts of electrocution. As the defense team pondered the facts, Scharrer invoked the law of nature. When one man steals another's wife, shouldn't his life be forfeit? Egan, the older member of the team, pointed out that the case would undoubtedly be tried under the law of Ohio rather than under the law of nature.

As he spoke, Egan's right hand suddenly dropped to his right hip pocket. Did that pocket contain a revolver? The money order ruse was obviously designed to bring Parker's wife to the telegraph office. The arrival of the wife's lover could not be predicted and was not designed by the information put by Parker on the money order. Egan's hand dropped again. Parker is standing in the shoeshine parlor and sees his wife's lover across the street. It was his chance to talk to him, to persuade him to mend his ways and let Parker take his wife back home to Savannah. Parker goes to the telegraph office. He approaches his wife's lover. Egan's hand drops again. Did Parker see his wife's lover make a move as if he planned to draw a weapon and attack? If so, was not the shooting in self-defense—an excusable homicide under Ohio law?

Whether or not self-defense was justified by the facts that unfolded at the postal telegraph office on the fatal morning, Egan was certainly correct about the instructions that would be given to a jury. The judge assigned to the case was Mason Douglass, a feisty lawyer from Alabama who served one term as a common pleas judge and then went back to a lengthy career as a trial lawyer who gave no quarter to his opponents and produced spellbinding rhetoric for his clients. When the evidence and arguments at the Parker trial came to a close, he gave the following guidance to the jury:

> The court charges the jury that there is no unwritten law in Ohio to the effect that a man may kill another man who has violated the chastity of his home through immoral relationship with his wife.

> Evidence has been produced in this case of extensive nature bearing upon the relation of Chestnut Payne to the wife of the defendant. The court charges the jury that regardless of how heinous and immoral the relationship of Chestnut Payne with the wife of the defendant Parker was, even though

it be entitled to the most severe condemnation, it in
itself could not under the law justify the defendant
in the killing of Payne.

After the verdict was returned Judge Douglass wryly noted that Parker was the first client with a good reputation ever represented by Jack Egan.

Several aspects of the trial and its preparation are of special interest to a trial lawyer practicing over eighty years later. We believe we live in a fast-moving world, yet justice now moves at a glacial pace compared to its pursuit in a day without computers or copy machines. On February 27, 1935, Parker was indicted on a charge of first degree murder which carried the potential of death in the electric chair. On March 1, 1935, Parker was arraigned and, shortly after they were appointed as his counsel, Egan and Scharrer on the same day sought a commission to take depositions in Savannah, Georgia, of twenty-two witnesses. In that application they were required to disclose the names, addresses and subjects of testimony of the proposed witnesses although the prosecution had no obligation to disclose anything concerning the state's witnesses who were located in Ohio. The trial began on April 1, 1935, just a month later. The lawyers had left Dayton on March 12. They had taken numerous depositions in Savannah and returned to Dayton on March 18. They then were engaged in the trial from March 28 to April 10, excluding only Sunday, March 31. In a little over ninety days from the incident the entire process was over.

In 1935, and well into the 1970s, there was no discovery in criminal cases in Ohio. Such cases went to trial without any pretrial disclosure of witnesses, exhibits or anything else. A trial lawyer had to have quick wits and fast feet. The only exception to the prevailing practice of trial by ambush and surprise was in the situation where testimony had to be preserved to be presented at trial because a witness was beyond the subpoena power of the court or otherwise unavailable to testify as a result of death, disease or some other extraordinary circumstance. In the Parker case, that posed a problem only for the defense counsel.

When the testimony of an out-of-state witness was preserved by a deposition taken in front of a special commissioner and reduced to a transcript, the practice at trial was to have one lawyer sit in the witness chair while another lawyer stood at the podium. The questions and answers would be read as the jury offered its auditory attention. The players were usually chosen for their histrionic skills in order to provide the reading some flavor of immediacy. Sometimes a picture of the witness would be displayed for the jury's visual consideration. This practice continued until well into the 1980s when it was gradually replaced by the presentation of testimony on video which was later played to a jury.

The practice of reading deposition transcripts was not as ineffective as it sounds. Video, like any "improvement" in the history of civilization, brought with it some negative qualities. Valuable time of lawyers and judges had to be consumed in the editing of objections and deletion of inadmissible testimony, sometimes leaving missing gaps or silent passages of some benefit to lip-reading jurors. And the video process could easily be sabotaged by interruptions which were difficult to edit out of a tape or by filibusters which left the presentation with a length that gave it all the excitement of the last hour of a marathon dance. To further enervate the process, jurors tended to treat the video presentation like they would their home television sets. As soon as the video started to play, its audience fell asleep. The more recent use of live testimony through video conferencing has brought an immediacy back to the process, and it has proved a vast improvement. Happily, in the 1930s when none of these technological advances had arrived, jurors who gathered information by reading and by listening to the radio actually paid attention to the sound of the human voice. I am sure that the jurors who encountered the deposition testimony in the Parker case absorbed each word as read despite the relative absence of tears and shouting-matches.

The Christmas Eve killing with its domestic triangle and its unusual preamble to death was a hot news item when the case came to trial in the spring of 1935. The defense team was already a local legend, and its preparation of the defense was becoming the legend of the local Bar. Despite the pressures of time the witness-gathering excursion to Savannah was not all drudgery. Egan always had a driver, and on the trip to Savannah he sat in the front passenger seat with his spittoon between his legs smoking his big Mike Ibold cigars while Scharrer occupied the back seat with the briefs and baggage. The road from Dayton to Savannah leads through

Kentucky and Tennessee and past innumerable hills and stills. Egan had the driver stop at the first likely looking backwoods restaurant, gathered together its three rural occupants, put two dollars on the table and offered to give it to them if they could divide it up. One took fifty cents, another took seventy-five cents. The third took seventy-five cents. "Nope," said Egan. "It has to be exactly equal." Faced with this perplexing problem, one of the fellows suggested that they take the two dollars, buy some moonshine with it, and divide the moonshine into three equal parts. This was a perfectly satisfactory solution for Egan, who shelled out another two dollars for a similar quantity of moonshine for himself and Scharrer.

This and similar ploys kept the defense team in high spirits and spiritous liquors during its investigative foray through the south. Meanwhile the prosecutorial team of Nick Nolan and Sam Kelly was all business, putting together a case that appeared impervious to any of the four elements. They had earned a reputation of unswerving commitment to seeking convictions in a world they regarded with zeal as divided between saints and sinners. It was the era when Dick Tracy entered the comics pages of newspapers across the country—a detective with sharply traced features and a girlfriend named Truehart. As Oscar Wilde once said, life imitates art just as art imitates life. The villains Tracy faced were all grotesque creatures of inhumanity with names no mother would give her child. They inhabited a world of utter blackness in contrast to the police world of pristine whiteness. Egan, as we have seen, saw all humans as citizens of a grey world in which the only difference between cops and robbers was the fact that the cops wore uniforms.

The house built by Nolan and Kelly was so well constructed that no flood could find a leak, no tornado could dislodge a shingle, no fire could penetrate a wall, no earthquake could shake its foundation. A jury was selected and sequestered at the Biltmore Hotel for the entire duration of the Parker trial. Opening statements were made, and despite Egan's endless gesture of dropping his hand to his right hip pocket—a gesture that almost drove Sam Kelly crazy—it looked like as good a case of premeditated murder as ever sent a felon to the electric chair. But was it unreasonable for Parker to think that there was a revolver in the right hip pocket of Parker's alleged victim?

The Parker jury.

The state's case opened with the clerk of the Ohio Hotel on Fifth Street who had registered Parker at 3:00 a.m. on December 24 as a hotel guest under the name of Davis Jones—an alias used by the prosecutors to suggest a premeditated Parker plan to consign his intended victim in seafaring terms to Davey Jones' locker. The next witness was a newspaper reporter from Savannah, Georgia who testified that Parker on resigning from the Savannah Police Force told the reporter that he would want Parker's picture before the year was out. The manager of the telegraph company then testified to the wire sent by Parker on December 22 authorizing the payment of ten dollars to Parker's wife, but instructing the company not to make payment until 9:00 a.m. on December 24. The clerk at the Ohio Hotel had testified that Parker left the hotel at 7:00 a.m. on the twenty-forth after leaving several requests to be called at 8:00 a.m.

Opening statements from both sides had confirmed that Parker had been waiting at a shoeshine stand at the entrance to the Dayton Arcade directly across Third Street from the postal telegraph company when Chestnut Payne and Mrs. Parker's mother arrived at Payne's fatal destination. The openings had also made it clear that Payne was a "crooner" who had been carrying on a love affair with Mrs. Parker. Fortunately for America's music-loving populace in the early 1930s, this crooner was not Bing Crosby.

After their scene-setting witnesses Nolan and Kelly called Payne's mother who confirmed that the crooner and Mrs. Parker had occupied the same bedroom on at least one occasion shortly before the killing. On cross-examination she identified pictures of her son and Mrs. Parker together, acknowledged that the two had been together over several months at her home in Kentucky, and that on one occasion the couple had come to Dayton where Chestnut bought a wedding ring for Mrs. Parker at a ten cent store. You could almost hear in the background Bing crooning "I Found A Million Dollar Baby In A Five and Ten Cent Store" from the wings of the courthouse.

Then the key witnesses took the stand in the persons of two female employees of the postal telegraph company. Their testimony could have been sung in unison since it was identical. They said that they were standing at the counter when Parker walked in, moved to within a foot of Payne's head and fired the first shot while saying "I told you I'd do it." They said that Payne never looked in Parker's direction and that, after the first shot, Parker fired a number of additional bullets into Payne's head.

Even Jack Egan could not come up with a magical cross-examination to undercut this testimony. Not that he didn't try. He tried in vain for two hours of wasted breath that produced nothing more than a minor inconsistency as to when one of the witnesses had given her statement to the coroner. At the end of Jack's valiant but futile effort, the last answer from the second witness was "I still say he did not turn around."

The next witness was a man who happened to be walking past the postal telegraph office on the morning of the shooting. He testified that he saw Parker emerge from the office, twirling the murder pistol around his fingers and then calmly rolling

Parker's mother-in-law and son on the day of the shooting.

a cigarette with one hand. Oh, dear! A police officer testified that he questioned Parker at the postal telegraph office and that during the questioning Parker was calm and unconcerned, rolling his cigarette with one hand. He claimed that Parker told him that he had quit his job on the Savannah Police Force purposely to come to Dayton and kill Payne and that he sent the telegram hoping to lure Payne to the office where he would see him. He also confirmed that Parker told him that, after the first shot, he walked back and shot Payne four more times to make sure he was dead.

If that was overkill, so was the testimony of two other police officers who said they heard Parker say that he had come a thousand miles to kill Payne. To confirm that Payne was not looking at Parker when he was shot, the former county coroner confirmed that the first shot struck Payne on the right side of his head and the other four shots struck him on the left side of his head. A big courtroom fight waged by Egan and Scharrer over the admissibility of some of the gruesome pictures managed to keep a few of them out of the jury's hands, but the testimony of the witnesses had to remain ringing in the jury's ears.

The last state's witness was the driver of an ambulance that had carried the body away. When he got back to the police station he commented to Parker "you did a good job of it." Parker allegedly replied, "I am satisfied. I came a thousand miles to kill that son of a bitch and it was a good thing my wife was not here or I would have killed her, too." As the curtain came down on the state's presentation, the background music shifted from Bing Crosby crooning a tune to Bessie Smith belting out "Send Me To The Electric Chair." At least so thought the thirteenth juror when he was discharged at the commencement of jury deliberations many days later. He told the press that his vote probably would have been guilty of first degree murder. When asked if Parker deserved the electric chair, he said "Well, it's pretty bad, pretty bad."

And now for the rest of the story. Undeterred in their quest for justice, Egan and Scharrer opened their defense by calling Parker's fifteen-year-old step-daughter as their first witness. She testified as to the numerous occasions when Payne had come to her mother's home for beer parties, wiener roasts and watermelon cuttings.

Kelly, still plagued by Egan's persistent hand-dropping gesture, objected to such testimony as having no bearing on the issue of self-defense. After heated arguments, Judge Douglass let the testimony be heard on the ground that it could have a bearing on the attitude of the accused. Deposition testimony from Savannah

Parker's step-daughter, his son, and Mrs. Parker on the day of the shooting.

witnesses as to Parker's good character was next on the defense agenda. Then it was time to light the fuse on the defendant's law of nature time bomb. A Savannah doctor who had examined Mrs. Parker on July 5, 1934, testified by deposition that she had a venereal disease and that his examination of Mr. Parker immediately thereafter showed that Mr. Parker was free from any venereal disease.

This testimony was followed by other depositions taken on Egan and Scharrer's trip to Savannah, adding more details to Mrs. Parker's illness from venereal disease after her cohabiting with her boyfriend, Chestnut Payne. There was also testimony concerning letters from Payne to Mrs. Parker, some salacious in content, others threatening Mr. Parker. There was also deposition testimony that Parker had been gassed when he was serving as a frontline dispatcher in General Pershing's Army in World War I and that he was nervous and threatening to commit suicide when he quit his job and left for Dayton.

Then poor Mrs. Parker was placed on the witness stand where she testified that Payne had threatened to kill Parker if Parker continued to interfere with their adulterous relationship. That testimony was drowned in buckets of tears and cataracts of contentions when Sam Kelly produced a written statement Mrs. Parker had given to the police several hours after the killing. Needless to say, that statement was not very favorable to the defendant. As Kelly went slowly and deliberately line-by-line through the statement, Mrs. Parker admitted that she said what was in the statement but claimed that she had been lying to the police in an attempt to protect Mr. Payne. After each answer she dissolved into sobs and from time to time

Mrs. Parker on the witness stand.

the jury had to be excused in an effort to permit her to regain some semblance of composure.

It is difficult to ascertain whether her testimony helped or hurt the defense. At the very least, it played right into the soap opera theme that invoked the law of nature. She ultimately testified that, while she loved Payne, she felt sorry for her husband who told her he would forgive and forget if she would return to live with him.

The last defense witness was the defendant Louis Parker. He testified on direct that he thought Payne was going for a gun and therefore shot him in self-defense. On cross by Kelly he responded to questions in a hesitating manner, and Kelly would ask another question before Parker had finished his answer. Egan continually interposed objections, asking that his client be permitted to finish his answers. Kelly demanded "yes" or "no" answers on cross-examination, and the fencing between the attorneys continued to build until Judge Douglass interposed and ruled that Parker had the right to finish his answers so long as his answers were pertinent to the questions. The fencing continued until Parker gave an answer that volunteered the statement that Payne had given his wife a venereal disease which she in turn had transmitted to Parker. At that point Kelly went through the courtroom ceiling, and all four attorneys entered into a screaming match that ultimately led Judge Douglass to excusing the jury while he put out the fire.

Kelly claimed that Egan had coached the witness to inject the claim which would justify the killing in the minds of the jurors. He demanded that the court order blood samples from both Mrs. Parker and Mr. Parker. Egan vehemently denied any wrongdoing on his part and insisted that his client's answer was responsive to the question posed by Kelly. He also accepted Kelly's blood test challenge with the comment "let us be mice or let us be men." Nolan and Scharrer joined in the shouting match. Judge Douglass announced that he was satisfied with the record and ordered a noon recess to permit a doctor to perform the requested blood tests.

Louis Parker on the witness stand, Judge Douglass and a court reporter.

In the afternoon court session the cross-examination of Parker continued at epic length, and every hot coal was raked over and over. The blood tests were positive for Mrs. Parker, but negative for Mr. Parker. At least it is consoling to find that he did not receive the case of syphilis that he claimed Payne had provided him through the agency of his wife. The state put the test results into evidence without objection from the defense. Egan's position was, whether or not Parker's wife had infected him, it was now clear beyond argument that Payne had infected Mrs. Parker.

The defense read the rest of the Savannah depositions, and tried to call another live witness who was excluded because he had not been identified before the state rested its case. Six hours were allotted to closing arguments. It was an era when people received information through their ears, and jurors—as well as galleries of spectators who had no televisions or smart phones to distract them or blunt their ability to absorb information—politely listened to the rhetoric of counsel presented to them without props or demonstrative tools. The trial had started on March 28. It went to the jury at noon on April 10. At 5:40 p.m. that evening a not-guilty verdict was returned. Mr. Parker went back to Savannah with his eight-year-old son (aptly named "Sunshine"). Mrs. Parker went to Florida to live with her mother. The lawyers went back to their respective offices.

SCENE 5:
America's Second Public Enemy No. 1

The defense verdict in the postal telegraph murder case did not dispel the vibrations from Jack's representation of Dillinger. Dillinger had been succeeded as Public Enemy Number One by Alvin Karpis, a member of the Barker-Karpis Gang. Karpis' claim to fame arose from highly publicized kidnappings and bank robberies. In May of 1935, the month following the postal telegraph verdict, he contacted Jack for some help in reducing the sentence imposed on his girlfriend, Dolores Delaney, who was serving time in the federal penitentiary in Milan, Michigan. Karpis described the contact in the autobiography he dictated after being paroled to Canada following a lengthy prison sentence in Alcatraz. Here is his account:

> I knew I'd never see Dolores again, but I made one last effort to help her. I read in the papers that she was convicted on three counts of harboring a criminal, namely, Alvin Karpis, and she was handed three five-year sentences. She couldn't even keep her baby. The poor kid. For a few moments in the hospital she held him in her arms and then he was given over to my parents. Dolores needed help, and at a fee of ten thousand dollars, I hired a lawyer in Dayton, Ohio to appeal her sentences. The lawyer's name was Jack Egan and he had a reputation as a first-rate appeals attorney. But he had no success in Dolores' case. As soon as he began preparations, the FBI descended on him. They tapped his phone, shadowed him, harassed him. They didn't know for sure that I was paying him,

but they suspected I was, and they wanted to scare him off the case. Eventually they succeeded. The appeal collapsed, and I realized that I would have to abandon Dolores the way I'd been forced to give up my wife, Dorothy.

According to government records, the "appeal" was designed to be a ten thousand dollar bribe to the sentencing judge for reconsidering and reducing the sentence that had been imposed on Dolores.

From Mary Hirsch in 1902 to Dolores Delaney in 1935, Jack was always ready to help a damsel in distress—or, if the occasion or client dictated, to push a damsel into distress. Poor Dolores, the sweetheart of Alvin Karpis, was left behind when Alvin with the help of a machine gun blazed his way out of a police trap at a small hotel in Atlantic City. Karpis and his accomplice Harry Campbell had been the subject of a manhunt for crimes ranging from robbery to kidnapping to murder. In 1934, Karpis and his gang had kidnapped Edward Bremer, a St. Paul, Min-

nesota banker. On that caper they obtained $200,000 in ransom money. The 1933 Karpis kidnapping of William A. Hamm, the president of Hamm's Brewery in St. Paul, had gleaned $100,000 in ransom money. Those crimes were simply the climax of a long series of bank robberies and other escapades.

Karpis and Campbell, along with their significant others, were in the fourth floor bedroom at the Dan-Mor hotel in Atlantic City when shortly before dawn on January 21, 1935, a bevy of police officers arrived at the hotel. Two of them went to the fourth floor and found the

Alvin Karpis.

Dolores Delaney.

door of the bedroom open. One of them poked a pistol through the opening and shouted "Stick 'em up. We're officers." Karpis shouted back "Stick 'em up yourself, copper. We are coming." As the door opened, Campbell grabbed a pistol. Karpis grabbed a machine gun. Bullets began flying. Karpis and Campbell got out of the room, stole a car, tried without success to rescue the two ladies left behind, and then engaged in a wild running gun battle with some twenty police officers through the streets of Atlantic City. The stolen car was later found, but Campbell and Karpis were gone.

The two ladies remained in police custody. Dolores had been shot in the leg during the initial gunfight. More significantly—and more dramatically—she was nearing the end of a pregnancy. On February 1, she gave birth to a seven-pound, four-ounce boy. She and the other lady, Wynonna Burdette, were held under $50,000 bail each by Florida authorities who would charge them with harboring felons. They were taken by federal officers, and accompanied by lots of luggage, to Miami, Florida on February 17. Dolores, whose leg still displayed a bandage over her bullet wound, had to leave the baby boy behind. Even taking into account the fur coat she was wearing on the trip, that is a pretty sad story. It got sadder on March 25, when both ladies were sentenced to five years in a federal penitentiary. The only happy note is that the baby was left in the tender care of Alvin Karpis' mother.

Dolores ended up in the federal penitentiary in Milan, Michigan, which was home to a number of ladies who had made similarly poor choices in their searches for mates. For commiserating company she had, among Wynonna and others, Evelyn Frechette who was one of Dillinger's girlfriends and Kathryn Kelly who was the wife of Machine Gun Kelly. On May 1, 1936, Alvin Karpis was captured by FBI agents in New Orleans without the firing of a shot. My sources don't recall what reaction Dolores Delaney had, if any, to the news report that Alvin was living with a pretty, red-haired twenty-one-year-old girl at the time of his arrest. Their neighbors described Alvin as a mild, pleasant man with a slight impediment to his speech and a significant interest in fishing. Just as Dolores got to know Kathryn Kelly in Milan, Michigan, Karpis in Alcatraz got to know Machine Gun Kelly who, believe it or not, was playing drums in the prison band organized by an excellent banjoist named Al Capone. I don't know if Karpis was part of that musical aggregation, but it is documented that Charlie Manson claimed to have learned how to play the guitar from Alvin when both were spending time in a California penitentiary. Music still soothes the savage breast.

On the bright side of the Delaney-Karpis romance, Alvin referred to a five-carat diamond ring taken from him on his arrest as "the only honest thing I own" and requested that it be put away for his son when the son grew up. When asked if he loved his son, he responded "How can you love something you have never seen?" He added, however, that his son wouldn't have to worry. "I've seen to it that Dolores Delaney won't worry for the rest of her life when she gets out." Whether that prediction turned out to be true has not been disclosed by the research which went into the preparation of these pages.

FBI records indicate that on May 17, 1935, Jack Egan called the clerk of the federal district court in Miami, Florida regarding the conviction of Dolores Delaney. In that time frame Jack and his wife had made a trip to Chicago, and Jack had made phone calls on May 10, 1935, and May 23, 1935, to Joe Roscoe, a Karpis confederate. On May 21, 1935, the FBI headquarters received a letter from its Jacksonville office regarding Jack's May 17 phone call. Obviously, the current Public Enemy Number One was at the center of the FBI target at this time, and anyone associated with him immediately became a person of interest. On July 5, 1935, Jack was interviewed by an FBI agent and indicated that his inquiry concerning Delores Delaney had merely been made "out of curiosity." That answer only sparked the FBI's curiosity about Jack Egan. Birnam Wood was heading toward Dunsinane Castle.

SCENE 6:
The Curtain Falls

As Karpis indicated, "the appeal collapsed." The FBI investigation of Jack, however, did not collapse. There were FBI interviews of Francis Canny who was the United States Attorney at Dayton, with Charlie Brennan who was at the time Dayton's Mayor, and with Si Yendes who was an inspector in the Dayton Police Department. The investigation finally came to a head on June 19, 1936 when a second FBI interview of Jack was undertaken. According to the agent, Jack "took a more or less hostile attitude" and refused to disclose anything about Delaney, Karpis or anyone or anything else. You can hear the echo of Macbeth: "Lay on Macduff and damned be he who cries 'hold enough'." The agent, in his report to J. Edgar Hoover, described Jack as "an old, experienced, capable criminal attorney…engaged as an underworld attorney." He noted that "it is difficult and also believed impossible to get any information out of him which would incriminate himself." "Seyton, my armor."

As Theseus discovered many centuries ago, it is easy to enter the labyrinth of life and experience, but it is a formidable—if not impossible—task to find your way out. Theseus needed Ariadne to give him a golden string to enable him to retrace his steps. Lady Macbeth had no golden string. She simply entered the labyrinth with her husband and went crazy. Nellie Egan appears to have decided not to enter the labyrinth. Instead she provided support from the outside to a husband who went deep into its depths. She had no golden thread to offer; only a kite string to grasp in what must have seemed a high and unflagging wind. Like all but one of those annual youths sacrificed by Athens, Jack Egan found only death at the end of the maze.

In June of 1936, Hoover had expressed a desire "to prosecute Egan on a harboring charge if possible, but if not, it will be well to scare him a little and make him think he is to be prosecuted on such a charge." It may or may not be considered coincidental that in May of 1936, the judge who handled the Delaney case had the dubious honor of being the first federal judge to be impeached by the United States Senate and removed from his "lifetime" position. On August 19, 1936, Jack at age sixty-three died unexpectedly of a heart attack. Among the honorary pallbearers at his funeral were Judge Roland Baggott, Judge Caroll Sprigg, Judge Robert Patterson, Irving Delscamp, Albert Scharrer, and other honored members of the Dayton Bench and Bar. They were appointed by Judge Don Thomas who at the time was President of the Dayton Bar Association and whose father for many years—including the day of the shoot-out on death row with Harry Pierpont and Charley Makley—had been the warden of the Ohio State Penitentiary.

As Walt Disney would say, it's a small world after all.

Egan grave site in Calvary Cemetery, Dayton, Ohio.

Epilogue—
Where's the Moral?

In every life there lurks a lesson. For Macbeth it proved the sad realization that we are all only poor actors strutting and fretting a fleeting hour upon the stage and that the paths of glory—like every other conceivable path—lead but to the grave. For Richard II it produced a similarly bleak rumination that no man who is no more than a man shall be pleased till he be eased with being nothing. Yet both Macbeth and Richard II remain vital and alive in memory, one for his runaway ambition and its corrosive effect on himself and others, the other for his ability to capture both his rise and fall in poetry. What thoughts and visions filled the mind of Jack Egan on his deathbed? Did all those past clients—from Andrew Spohr and Dayton Slim through Crane Neck Nugent and Jew Bates to John Dillinger and Alvin Karpis—parade through his bedroom and ask him, like Richard III, to despair and die? Or did he simply smile back at it all and relish the life experience in which he had encountered more characters than Chaucer had pilgrims or Falstaff had barflies.

In a search for meaning in Jack Egan's life or in any other life, the best guide may be the centuries-old Aunt Ester, a creation of the great American playwright August Wilson. A disillusioned young man comes to her for wisdom and advice. His search for a meaningful life has led him to the conclusion that life has no meaning. "Whoever told you that it is supposed to have meaning?" asks the old woman, "It's a mystery and an adventure, and that's enough." Aunt Ester's name, as countless critics have noted, sounds phonetically like "ancestor," thereby suggesting that

141

the path to wisdom leads the mental traveler into the past. If we go all the way back to Herodotus, the father of history, we learn that history is not simply a succession of events. Its purpose is to ensure that the deeds of men be not forgotten. Good men and bad men, strong or weak, funny or depressing, lovable or despicable, dignified or disorganized, rich or poor, white or black or red or yellow, subjects of envy or subjects of scorn—all those lives teach us our own humanity.

Like those lives, like yours, like mine, the life of Jack Egan reflects both the meaninglessness of earthly existence and its ultimate meaning as a wonderful and miraculous experience of mystery and adventure. And I hope that, for you as well as for me, that's enough.

There is an old New Orleans funeral song about a colorful character who rambled until the butchers cut him down. Jack was lucky. Fueled by vaulting ambition, energy, humor, and evolving cynicism, he certainly rambled through his career. Fate cut the cord of his earthly existence before the butchers (who were waiting at the door) cut him down. But, didn't he ramble?

On Sunday, April 9, 1865, unaware that Grant and Lee at that moment were working out surrender terms at Appomattox Courthouse, President Lincoln and his entourage were returning to Washington by boat from City Point. Lincoln spent several hours reading passages from *Macbeth* to the group. Apparently Mrs. Lincoln made a mental connection between Shakespeare's Scottish usurper and the leader of the American rebellion. Out of the blue at the close of her husband's reading she made the observation that Jefferson Davis ought to be hanged. In response Lincoln said "Judge not that ye be not judged."

In Dayton in 1936, the leaves had all fallen. Jack Egan, a man of boundless imagination, had come to the end of imagination. Had he—like the headless Macbeth—come to a plain sense of things, inanimate in an inert savoir? Does his colorful life provide for you, dear Reader, an inevitable knowledge, required as necessity requires? Are he, you and I blessed by a God who is, after all, merciful?

Acknowledgments

Judge Michael W. Krumholtz of the Common Pleas Court of Montgomery County—a fine jurist who in his days before ascending the Bench was given a high state accolade as a model of professional ethics—was the source of the description of Jack Egan's funeral that opens this little book. He got the story from his father who was one of the attendees at that event.

Thirty years of conversations and interviews with lawyers and judges who practiced in Dayton in the first third of the twentieth century have added another layer to this book. Some of that layer has previously appeared in a history of Dayton's Bench and Bar which I published in 1996, the 200th year from the founding of Dayton. I gave the book a title familiar to those who drink deeply at Walt Whitman's Pierian Spring. Unfortunately, the title inspired little more than surprised and confused glances from those who occupied its potential marketplace. Used copies can now be acquired at give-away prices on Amazon.com.

The bedrock of this book comes from the enthusiastic and assiduous research of Denise M. Testa, a fan of Jack Egan who came upon him in her own quest to know all there is to know about Charley Makley, the member of the Dillinger gang who hailed from northwest Ohio where her maternal grandmother recited stories of him and the gang. She has scoured the internet, FBI files, old newspapers, documents, books, and articles to glean all there is to know on our subject. Together we have visited Jack's childhood home in Excello, the graves of his mother and sister in Middletown, his hideaway home in Randolph Township, the graves of him and his wife, Nellie, in Calvary Cemetery in Dayton. We have gathered old photographs and taken new photographs, and we have shared the pleasure of getting to know a ghost who comes to life through repeated visitations. My thanks—and hopefully yours—belong to Denise without whose prodding these pages would have remained blank.

My companion in jazz (and an artist of dazzling skill), Greg Dearth, with some assistance from his talented wife, Liz, provided the cover art for this volume. The task of transforming my scribbles and dictation into print was ably handled by Jennie Ladd, while Deni Ryan helped with the pictures which are embedded in the text. Both have been my friends and able assistants for years. Jennie began her career with William Mayfield, a legendary local photographer who provided images of Dayton as it existed in Jack Egan's era. She went on to become the administrative assistant in charge of Stan Kenton's jazz band, and, thereafter, secretary to various members of the Dayton Bar—an excellent training ground for supporting a lawyer-musician (or is it musician-lawyer?).

Finally, thanks are due to my wife, Dulie, who, while she cares little about Jack Egan, cares much about me. With infinite patience and never a harsh word, she has put up with, humored, and supported a husband who spends his waking hours consumed in trying lawsuits, playing jazz, reading arcane books, and spouting war stories fueled by beer. For decades we have shared love, affection, friendship, understanding and the same mindset on politics and the meaning (or lack thereof) of life. Who could ask for anything more?

The Theaters in which Jack Egan Performed from 1899 to 1936

Montgomery County Jail, 1874–1965

North side of Third Street, between Main and Ludlow.

Dayton City Workhouse, 1874–1933

Northwest corner of Sixth and Main streets.

"New" Montgomery County Courthouse, 1874–1966

West side of Main Street between Second and Third streets.

City Police Court and Jail, 1873–1913

South side of Sixth Street, just west of Tecumseh Street.

City Municipal Court and Jail, 1913–1953

East side of Main Street, between Third and Fourth streets.

Index

F

FBI, Federal Bureau of Investigation, 134, 137–138

Fairbanks, Douglas, 120

Faulkner, William, 5

Ferneding, Judge H.L., 97

Fields, W.C., 58, 72, 113

First Baptist Church, 17

Fishbach, William R., 36, 39, 47–48

Flannery, James, 64

Flynn, Errol, 120

Ford, Rodney, 100–102

Foutz, Earl, 60

Fowler, Roy, 63–64

Fragonard, Jean-Honoré, 27

Fraternal Order of Eagles, 55

Fraternal Order of Oaks Club, 78–79

Frechette, Billie, 121, 136

French Lick Springs, 56

G

Garden of Allah, 116

General Motors, 5, 114

Gilman, Donna, 22

Gondorf, Charlie, 72

Gondorf, Fredrick, 71–73, 112–113

Gondorf, George, 72

Gottschall, Oscar, 17

Gottschall, Turner & Carr, 58

Grand Hotel, 116

Grapewin, Charley, 44

H

Hagelganz, Fannie, 61

Hagelganz, Henry, 61–62, 90

Hagerty, Mayme, 63

Hall, Warren, 46

Hallanan, Walter, 43

Hamilton, Polly, 121

Hamm, William A., 135

Harding, Warren G., 73–74

Harries, Lizzie, 57

Hatcher, Doctor, 39, 44–45

Hawthorne Smoke Shop, 108

Hecht, Fred W., 81–82

Heck, Frank J., 78

Hedges, Lib, 18, 29

Heindel, Carl, 101

Hemingway, Ernest, 5

Herodotus, 142

Hirsch, Mary, 21, 135

Hollencamp, Henry, 33

Hoop De Doos, 56

Hoover, J. Edgar, 6, 94, 117, 138

Hotel Gibson, 68

Howell, Dick, 94

Hur, Ben, 21

I

Indiana State Reformatory, 117

Indiana State Prison (Michigan City), 117–118

J

Jacobs, "Turkey Joe," 103–104

James, Harry P., 79

Jeffrey, Harry, 85

Jones, Moses, 30

Jordan, Charlie, 27

Joyce, James, 5

K

Karl, George (aka "Jew" Bates), 108

Karpis, Alvin, 22, 134–138, 141

About the Author and Researcher

AUTHOR DAVID C. GREER has been a practicing trial lawyer in Dayton, Ohio, for fifty-five years. He has represented clients in more than five hundred jury trials, ranging from capital murders to corporate takeovers and including medical and legal malpractice and ethics; patent disputes; contract and commercial disputes of all kinds; white-collar and blue-collar and no-collar criminal charges; and cataclysmic injuries resulting from electrocutions, explosions, train wrecks, highway accidents, product mishaps, drugs and chemicals. Those adventures have taken place throughout Ohio as well as in Illinois, Minnesota, California, Colorado, Indiana, Kentucky, Missouri and Georgia. He has been a Fellow of the American College of Trial Lawyers and Life Member of the Sixth Judicial Circuit since the late 1970s.

While appreciative of Jack Egan's skills, the author asserts that he has not modeled his own career on that of the subject of this work. He is the author of a history of the Dayton bench and bar from 1796 to 1996, and he is the leader of an eight-piece jazz band which has carried the great music of the 1920s and 1930s to a variety of venues for almost forty years.

David C. Greer

Denise M. Testa.

DENISE M. TESTA is responsible for most of the intensive research that went into this book. She has proven herself an energetic and enthusiastic paragon among fact detectives and archaeologists of arcane history.

Her curiosity of Jack Egan began while reading of a rumor about a bribe which involved Jack Egan and a member of the Dillinger gang. At the time, the rumor seemed far-fetched but she decided to follow-up on it, leading her to the expert on all things Egan—David C. Greer. Together, the more they collectively dug, the more twists and turns the tale took. It became apparent that these great stories needed to be shared with a new audience.

Denise is resident of western New York and has been practicing veterinary medicine for over twenty years with a specialty in Canine Rehabilitation. Her writing experience is based mainly with peer-reviewed papers presented at Auburn University, University of Minnesota, and North Carolina State University, as well as local institutions. She shares a home with four-legged and two-legged friends.